THE TIES THAT BIND

"IDENTIFYING & BREAKING UNHEALTHY SOUL TIES"

Brian A. Holmes

BLAZE
PUBLISHING
MANSFIELD, TEXAS

W9-BCA-014

THE TIES THAT BIND by Brian A. Holmes
Published by Blaze Publishing House
A division of Ministry Solutions, LLC
P.O. Box 184
Mansfield, TX 76063
www.msicreative.com
www.blazepublishinghouse.com

Unless otherwise noted, all Scripture quotations are from the New American Standard – Updated Version of the Bible. Copyright © 1960, 1962, 1963, 1968, 1971, 1972, 1973, 1975, 1977 by the Lockman Foundation. Used by permission.

Scripture quotations marked KJV are from the King James Version of the Bible. Copyright © 1979, 1980, 1982 by Thomas Nelson, Inc., publishers. Used by permission.

Scripture quotations marked AMP are from the Amplified Version of the Bible. Old Testament Copyright © 1965, 1987 by the Zondervan Corporation. The Amplified New Testament copyright © 1954, 1958, 1987 by the Lockman Foundation. Used by permission.

Scripture quotations marked MSG are taken from THE MESSAGE. Copyright © 1993, 1994, 1995, 1996, 2000, 2001, 2002. Used by permission of NavPress Publishing Group.

Library of Congress Catalog Card Number: PCN 2008920163
ISBN-13: 978-0-9792071-1-2
ISBN-10: 0-9792071-1-8

BRIAN A. HOLMES
MINISTRIES

I dedicate this book to my precious family. For many years, they have sacrificed much and paid a heavy price so that I could do what God has called me to do. I could never adequately express how blessed I am to have each of them as a part of my world.

To my wife, Sabrina:

My friend, my lover, my partner, the mother of our children, and my greatest supporter. Thank you for allowing me to travel the world and seeing in me what I cannot see in myself. I love you with all of my soul!

To my son, Christian:

You are the apple of my eye. I am blessed and favored of God to have a son so powerful, so talented, and so tender. Follow your dreams and be the man God has created you to be. I am proud of you; I believe in you; and I love you with all my heart.

To my daughter, Abigail:

You are "your father's joy"! I could never have asked for a more beautiful and precious gift than what God has given me in you. You are a blessing and a breath of fresh air to all you come in contact with. I am proud to be your "boyfriend." Daddy loves his little girl!

Acknowledgments

In one's lifetime, there are many people that shape, influence, and impact a life. My life has been no exception. I have been blessed by God to have had many precious people pour into me, pray for me, and speak into me; making me the man I have become. I would like to acknowledge some of those individuals here.

To my mother, Evelyn Holmes. Your prayers and your love have literally saved me more times than I could ever count. Your guidance and your direction have been a priceless asset and blessing. Your and Dad's examples taught me to care for people. I thank you, I love you, and I will forever be indebted to you for your sacrifice and love

To Bishop Tudor Bismark. How can I express the measure of influence and defining impact you have had on my life, as well as that of our ministry? God graced me with the opportunity to serve you and ChiChi, but in reality, I have received the greatest blessing. Thank you for allowing me the opportunity to learn at your feet and thank you for sharing with us the greatness that is in you. I love you and honor you.

To Bishop Richard Heard. It is amazing to consider how God arranged events and circumstances so that you and I could come into such a relationship. You are a true mentor and an incredible friend. Your genuine, heart-felt concern and love for us has been, and is, one of the greatest blessings we have ever received in our lives. Thank you for your love, your counsel, and your commitment to me as a son. I am proud and blessed to call you, "Father."

To Bishop Joseph Garlington, Sr. For many years, you mentored me through audio tapes without even realizing it. During the last ten years, I have been privileged to have you in mine and Sabrina's life as a counselor, a friend, and a loving supporter of what we are endeavoring to do. Thank you for being there for us and for showing us a living example and model of reconciliation and multicultural ministry.

To Bishop Jack "PaPa" DeHart. When my dad passed away, you stepped in as a wonderful and loving father figure in my life. You have always affirmed me, loved me, and shown me the way to be a man of integrity and vision. Thank you for your willingness to always be honest and share the many years of wisdom with which God has endowed you.

To all my friends and family. You have encouraged me and pushed me to pursue my dreams and be who God has called me to be: THANK YOU!

To my CIWC family. I am honored and blessed that God has chosen Sabrina and I to shepherd and lead such an incredible group of people. Thank you for allowing me to do all that I do. Thank you for seeing the vision and being willing to take the journey with me!

Table of Contents

Foreword

by Bishop Tudor Bismark

We live in a day where Satan is busy trying to keep God's people—the legitimate sons of God in the earth—restricted and limited in their ability to achieve their "God-purpose" in this life. While spiritual warfare has many dimensions to it, ultimately the objective is to move demonic dominance and to CHALLENGE demonic influences operating in the lives of God's people. Understanding this, we must first deal with the element of humanity, as it relates to God's workings in the earth. Human beings are generally enslaved to demonic systems and influences because of words, deeds, or relationships that have given Satan a legal and legitimate position with which he can hold an individual captive. Soul ties are one of the major areas through which Satan can wreak havoc in one's life. Whether an individual is aware of their presence or not, they can cause deep and long-lasting wounds that handicap a person spiritually, physically, emotionally, relationally, and even economically. These soul ties, then, bind people to this world of evil, resulting in dramatic repercussions, and in many cases, never-ending cycles that leave the individual empty and unfulfilled.

In this book, Brian has captured the true essence of deliverance, counseling, rehabilitation, and inner healing. *The Ties That Bind* clearly and accurately deals with the concept of soul ties; giving the reader the knowledge and understanding necessary to bring to light what is holding them back. You will understand the classes of soul ties, their effects, and how they operate and control areas of your life. *The Ties That Bind* also establishes a position that will ultimately destroy generational curses and release generational blessings. This book provides a powerful step-by-step approach that will help you identify and isolate those areas where freedom and release is needed and will walk you through the process of repenting, renouncing, and becoming free in all areas of your life.

This is really a Kingdom position and a Kingdom model for dealing with soul ties. I wholeheartedly commend this book to you as a powerful tool to be used in your journey to freedom and effectiveness.

Introduction to Soul Ties

"I just can't ever seem to get beyond a certain point."

"Every time I seem to be getting ahead, something happens to yank the carpet out from under me again."

"It just seems like every relationship I have ends up hurting me and leaving me empty."

"Why am I like this?"

I have heard these statements, and others like them, hundreds of times over years of serving in ministry. Why is it that Believers—born-again, children of God—seem to be in as bad of shape, if not worse, than unbelievers? Why is it that church-going, tithe-paying, Sunday-school-working, committed Christians seem to deal with the same kinds of issues as nonbelievers? Why is it that even pastors and church leaders from every denomination, every part of the world, and every conceivable social class, carry hidden sins, secret struggles, wounded hearts, and tormented minds for years; many of whom never know what it means to be truly free, happy, and fulfilled?

I do not pretend to have all the answers, but I do know this: my own life is a testimony of someone who was afforded many advantages and blessings in my early years, and yet I carried deep struggles that no one, not even those closest to me, really knew about. Whose fault was this? Who could I blame? Where could I point my finger? The answer, believe it or not, was fairly simple.

The Bible teaches that we are destroyed, or perish, because of a lack of knowledge (Hosea 4:6). Let's consider this for a moment.

The definition of "perish" is *to pass from existence; disappear gradually; to spoil or deteriorate; to suffer destruction or ruin.*

There's an old saying that goes something like this: "What you don't know can't hurt you." But on the contrary, I submit to you that what you don't know CAN DESTROY YOU! The Bible is clear that without knowledge we are sure to waste away, be undone, cease to be, and eventually die, having never come to the fullness God intended for our lives. We must have knowledge!

I grew up in and around a church environment all my life. I was taught many guiding principles from the Bible, and have always considered myself a student of God's Word. What I have come to realize in the last number of years is that God's knowledge is infinitely greater than any theology or doctrine to which I might subscribe. Knowledge—true knowledge—goes far beyond Sunday school, a textbook, a seminary, or even a Sunday morning sermon. There is so much more He wants to reveal to us, if we will only open our hearts to receive and embrace it.

God is omniscient. Webster defines "omniscient" as *having infinite awareness, understanding, and insight; possessed of universal or complete knowledge.* That's the God I serve. To seek knowledge is to seek Him. To embrace new revelation and new understanding is to come into a closer and more intimate relationship with God. The closer I get to Him, the more I receive healing and restoration and freedom!

The book you hold in your hands contains information concerning a topic I believe is systemic in nature and can explain why people are bound, hurting, and unnecessarily restricted in the progress of their lives' purposes. Throughout these chapters, I will take you on a journey of information, which I pray will be translated by the Holy Spirit into revelation, so that you will come to a place of freedom and healing you never knew possible.

THE TOPIC: SOUL TIES

In the following pages, you will learn how it is entirely possible to be saved, filled with God's Spirit, and living a good life, and yet still be bound by addictions, behaviors, poverty, sickness, and other destructive elements. Satan has one objective: the annihilation of Mankind in general and of your life, in particular. To achieve his objective, he operates using a three-fold strategy: to steal from you, to kill you, and to destroy you (John 10:10). He wants to steal your happiness, steal your dreams, and steal your ability to believe what God believes about you. He wants to kill the effectiveness, the creativity, the power, and the potential with which you have been eternally endowed by God. He wants to destroy your future before you ever have the pleasure of seeing it fulfilled. He is all about affecting your life in ways that cause you to never be able to find true fulfillment, true happiness, and the realization of God's destiny and purpose in your life. Understanding this, it is important that we establish a few key premises:

1. Because God is a just and legal God, Satan can only affect your life to the degree that he has *legal* right to do so.

2. He will use any and all means to derail you from the path God has chosen for your life. When it comes to his strategies and schemes, it's gloves off.

3. Old relationships, encounters, and alliances CAN and WILL continue to affect every area of your life until they have been resolved by the application of the blood of Jesus and the undoing of soul ties made as a result of those relationships.

Let me give you a general definition of soul ties at this point. (We will be describing and exploring them in greater detail a little later.) Soul ties are formed through relationships, connections, and covenants we make throughout the course of life. These "connections" tie us to people, places, churches, and other entities, and they can dramatically affect our lives. Satan uses this tool as a means to control our progress in all areas of life.

The bottom line ... **God wants you free!** The key is this: you have to want to be free, for yourself. It has to be *your* desire, *your* will, and *your* determination to achieve freedom. Paul said it this way: *". . . Forgetting what lies behind and reaching forward to what lies ahead,"* (Philippians 3:13). It is impossible to reach your future while being tied to your past. It is impossible to embrace something fresh and new if you are holding onto things that are old and have long ago exceeded their worth and usefulness in your life. These are choices that each of us make as we enter this process.

I challenge you today, as you read through these pages, to open your heart to the Lord's voice. As you go through each chapter, allow Him to reveal to you those areas where you are tied and bound by unhealthy spiritual alliances—or soul ties— you may have formed consciously or unwittingly throughout your life.

My prayer for you is that you experience the freedom and joy of being released into God's full destiny and plan for your life. Take the journey. It really is worth it!

Section I

A Journey
of the
Soul

CHAPTER 1

The Journey Begins

There are numerous reasons why someone would pick up a book like this one. In today's world, there are far too many people who are worn-out and frustrated with their lives. They seem to have no direction, no stability, feel very little significance and even less value. Maybe this describes someone you know—or maybe this describes you. Are you tired of constantly being held back? Have you found yourself asking these questions:

- ♦ *Why can't I ever get ahead?*

- ♦ *What's wrong with me?*

- ♦ *Why does "this" keep happening to me?*

- ♦ *Why do I seem to live in such a hellish mess all the time?*

- ♦ *Why does my life seem so limited and lethargic?*

You have more questions than answers. For months, maybe even years, you have wandered around aimlessly like the children of Israel did for forty years trying to find their "Promised Land." Others around you are progressing, getting ahead, and getting promotions, yet there are areas in your life where it seems like you take five steps forward and three steps back—or worse, one step forward and five steps back.

> There are legitimate reasons why you continue to be drawn back into the same old mess, wrestle with the same demons, and achieve the same results over and over again.

Maybe you're just tired of being sick and tired. To describe your life as "dysfunctional" would actually be a step up from where you feel you are now—not functioning at all. Desperate for real solutions, you are searching for something or someone who holds the key that will unlock the cyclical prison where you continually find yourself.

Let's begin by building on this premise: there are legitimate reasons why you continue to be drawn back into the same old mess, wrestle with the same demons, and achieve the same results over and over again. You must understand that God is a legal God, and the systems that govern our existence operate within the confines of legality and providence. In other words, the things that work adversely against us have a legal right to do so, and our job is to discover what they are and how to undo them.

These forces are real and they are powerful. They carry weight and have the ability to hinder, or even stop altogether, the progress and journey of our lives. One of the most common and most harmful causes for these patterns is *soul ties*. Without a doubt, ungodly and unhealthy soul ties could very well be the reason you feel as if hell itself has been unleashed on your life. It could be that there are soul ties at work in your life that have limited you, tied you down, and governed your life without you even knowing that they exist.

It is my sincere belief that in some area of each of our lives, right now, every one of us is dealing with the effects of soul ties in some way. That's right; I said every one of us. As we walk out the process of growing in our relationship with God, He continuously reveals areas that we must address and deal with.

It is important to note here that not all soul ties are ungodly or unhealthy. In fact, in the context of right and Godly relationships, soul ties can be very positive and beneficial to our lives. Ungodly and unhealthy soul ties, however, will affect us adversely and rob us of our joy in living for Him.

> ... a soul tie can lie dormant within you and remain completely under the radar, without showing any signs or giving any indications that it is present.

This is the area we must focus on as God helps us to break free.

I have mentioned the concept of soul ties several times, and will provide you with an in-depth definition and teaching in a later chapter, but in general terms, an ungodly or unhealthy soul tie is a *soulish* disease. As you will learn, the soul is that part of us that houses our emotions, memories, intellect, habits; in short, all those non-physical, non-spiritual parts of us that make us unique. For years, a soul tie can lie dormant within you and remain completely under the radar, without showing any signs or giving any indications that it is present. But like other diseases, soul ties eventually begin to produce noticeable symptoms. As with diseases of the human body, some symptoms are immediately evident, while others may be affecting your quality of life without you fully recognizing it. The latter is often the case with soul ties. They quietly and inconspicuously affect the patterns of your life, and ultimately determine your ability to produce and/or progress in life.

Have you ever known anyone who ignored physical symptoms for too long, only to be later diagnosed with a major illness? Almost without exception, their doctor will say something like, "If we had only caught this earlier, we would have had a much better chance of a treatment and cure." The reality of this scenario takes place all the time, and is tragic and unnecessary.

The same can be said of soul ties. Even if soul ties are not wreaking havoc in your life right now, they may covertly and in a stealth-like way be keeping you from realizing and accomplishing your dreams and fulfilling your destiny and purpose in life.

The reason many individuals are never able to experience and walk in the fullness of the promises of God for their lives is because they are tied to things and/or people whose influence in their life is a liability, not an asset. Their souls are connected in a way that prohibits them from discovering creativity and achieving the momentum and power to successfully forward. They find themselves unable to step into the river of the abundant flow of God's blessings. It's as though they are teetering on the edge of the bank, desiring to plunge into the fullness of God's purpose for them, but something or someone—known or not known—has them anchored to a past action, thought, or memory; keeping them locked into a present reality that is less than what God intends.

CLOSING THOUGHTS

My friend, don't be afraid to allow God to expose in you areas in which you may be ensnared by a soul tie. Remember, *"God has not given us the spirit of fear, but of power, and love, and of a sound mind,"* (2 Timothy 1:7, NKJV).

Decide right now to trust God. Choose in this moment to know that He will help you. If you ask the Holy Spirit to reveal these areas of hindrance to you, He absolutely will. He wants more than anything for you to be free so He can take you somewhere. He has predestined your life. *"Before I formed you in the womb I knew you, and before you were born I consecrated you,"* (Jeremiah 1:5). There is a predetermined eternal script for your life, which God set in place before the foundations of the world.[1] He wants to give you everything you have ever desired. As a matter of fact, He is the originator of those desires in you; He put them there to begin with.

As for me, I don't want to be held back! I have determined to no longer allow religious mindsets, traditions, what men think, or anything else keep me from receiving everything God intends for me. I don't want to just stick my big toe into this powerful river of God's abundant life; I want to dive in over my head and be carried by the flow of the power and abundance of what God has prepared for me. I want to experience the real purpose for my life and walk out the perfect plan He has for me. I want access to every promise God has given me and to the Kingdom life that I am designed to live. I believe if you are reading this book, you want that, too!

> Wherever you are . . . right now, . . . it is not too late for you. God knows your name! He has made a way for to get off this roller-coaster once and for all . . .

Please, know this: wherever you are in your journey right now, at whatever level

---

[1] "Then the King will say to those on His right, 'Come, you who are blessed of My Father, inherit the kingdom prepared for you from the foundation of the world,'" (Matthew 25:34).

or stage of development and healing, it is not too late for you. God knows your name! He has a vested interest in seeing you whole: body, soul, and spirit. He has made a way for you to get off this rollercoaster once and for all, and to begin to live with peace, joy, and hope again. Help is on the way!

CHAPTER 2

The Basis for Change

Changing Our Mind Changes Our World

For the past several years now, Believers have begun to realize that the Church has been ineffective at addressing many of the issues that plague our world. We have perfected the message of "going to the next level"—and we've preached it hard. It's become as clichéd as the coined phrase, "God is good," with the congregation responding right on cue, "All the time." Still, as Believers we reach a certain point of progress in our life only to find ourselves hitting an invisible ceiling, and that "next level" seems unattainable, out of our reach.

WHERE WE ARE NOW

What does it really mean to be a Believer? Are we any different from the rest of the world? Is there truly an advantage to walking with God? Or, are our lives destined for the same challenges, disappointments, and struggles as those who don't even know Christ?

I want to submit this to you for thought. While we are saved, redeemed, justified, sanctified, and cleansed—*and we are*—many of us, as individuals, find ourselves walking out our lives having the same measure and standard of results as do our unsaved counterparts in the world. I have traveled the world and have been in hundreds of churches from many different streams and camps. What I have observed is consistent everywhere I go.

> In the Church, there are just as many on antidepressants, being treated by therapists, and dealing with deep emotional issues as outside the Church.

So many Believers are depressed, dazed, defeated, and financially depleted; continually unable to break through the obstacles that oppose them. In the Church, there are just as many on antidepressants, being treated by therapists, and dealing with deep emotional issues as outside the Church. The truth is, despite all the hype and hoopla and all of the religious ceremony, the majority of the Body of Christ has demonstrated little progress in the area of developing and healing the soul.

Family Life. The divorce rate among born-again Christians equals that of non-believers and non-churchgoers; making long, until-death-do-us-part, monogamous, and fulfilling marriages almost extinct. Our children don't stand out from the world; instead they are being conditioned and programmed to blend into secular society and culture. They listen to the same music, watch the same movies and television, talk the same language, and are gradually being conformed into the world's standards of fashion and lack of modesty.

Church Life. The Church in the Western world finds itself at a difficult crossroads. Even though many attend church on a regular basis, their spiritual lives are fragmented and weak. We love God, but do we have a meaningful and unrestricted relationship with Him? Like so many, we have lost our "first love" and no longer serve God with the same drive and intensity we once did.

> Even though many attend church on a regular basis, their spiritual lives are fragmented and weak.

Spiritual Life. Since being saved and born again, many Believers find themselves on a spiritual rollercoaster; going from spiritual highs on Sunday mornings to plummeting to the lows of questioning if their relationship with God is secure and in a healthy place by Tuesday evening. The Church has created a culture of spiritual dependency. Christians continue to be fed "you can make it" messages, but never are given the tools to be healed in their souls.

Financial Life. We can preach and talk the prosperity Kingdom message, but our checkbooks have more bounce on them than a jumbo trampoline. We're in debt up to our eyeballs and mortgaged to the hilt. Financially, we can't freely obey God to give when we see a need because we're barely living from paycheck to paycheck, week to week; struggling financially ourselves.

Ministry Life. Every year, more and more ministers of the Gospel are leaving the work of ministry because of moral failure, wrecked marriages, a loss of purpose and focus, or because they are just flat-out discouraged and worn-out in the fight, tired of living in turmoil and pain.

Most of the time, church folk find themselves struggling with the same issues as those who have not given their lives to God. This cannot be the way God intended it! It makes no sense at all. You might be reading this and saying to yourself, "This is such a negative way to look at things. Surely, things are not *that* bad." Open your eyes! The Body of Christ can no longer afford to embrace the simplistic "feel-good" philosophy of *"I'm okay, you're okay,"* as a universal cure-all for the deteriorating condition of society in general and the Church, in particular. You see, we may be saved and committed to God on many levels, but we still wrestle with the same issues year in and year out. How can we break this cycle? How can we get off of this merry-go-round that is going nowhere? We must come to a place of honesty and transparency, as individuals, and allow God to begin to reveal to us the way of change.

I want to say again that there are legitimate and causative reasons why this all-too-common pattern is seen throughout the Body of Christ. There is no doubt in my mind that one of the reasons we cannot break through, break free, and move forward is because we are being held captive by unhealthy and ungodly soul ties. We are tied to systems, relationships, individuals, ideas, and thoughts that keep us immobilized and incapable of moving into God's best.

DISCERNING THE SEASON

Fortunately, that is not the end of the story! Ecclesiastes 3:1 tells us that to every thing there is a season.[2] God's desire is to release to His global, corporate Body one of the most prosperous and powerful seasons the world has ever seen. However, in order to position ourselves to move into this season of power and demonstration, there are some things we must address in order to be qualified and prepared. We must be liberated—spirit, soul, and body—to move into that next dimension, both on an individual level and as a corporate body. It is imperative that, as Believers, we begin to learn and understand:

> God's desire is to release to His global, corporate Body one of the most prosperous and powerful seasons the world has ever seen.

---

[2] "There is an appointed time for everything. And there is a time for every event under heaven," (Ecclesiastes 3:1).

1. What soul ties are and how they work;

2. How to identify and recognize them operating in our own lives;

3. How to effectively and legally break them from of our lives forever.

WHAT'S BEHIND DOOR NUMBER 3?

Many years ago in the United States, there was a television game show called, "Let's Make a Deal." Each week, contestants would compete for a chance to have the option to choose between three doors, behind one of which would be a marvelous set of prizes. These prizes were usually high-ticket items such as new cars, boats, and motor homes; vacation packages and expensive jewelry—the list was long and varied.

Just imagine that you are the contestant with the choice to make. Your choice: Door Number 3. The host says loudly, "Show us what's behind Door Number 3!" You hear the announcer excitedly shout, "It's a brand-new car!" The crowd goes wild and you are overcome with emotion and excitement. You lose all inhibitions and with your arms flailing around in disbelief, you scream, "Thank you, Jesus! I just won a brand-new car!! Can you believe it?" There's one slight problem—you are blind.

All around you, there are shouts of excitement. You can reach out and touch your new car. You can even feel what it's like to sit in the driver's seat and put your hands around the steering wheel—but you'll never be able to drive it. You can even go so far as to put the key in the ignition, fire up the engine, and hear the pistons hammering away. You experience all the emotions, all the sensations, all the hype, but you do not possess the ability to carry your experience to the ultimate level. You will never experience firsthand what it is like to personally drive that car. You will never know the satisfaction of starting at point "A" and arriving at your destination.

This is exactly where many believers find themselves today. God has set before us an open door. Our blessings, promotions, wealth and prosperity, business success, health, happiness, and dreams are right in front of us. We can imagine the excitement. We can smell the aroma of victory. We can practically touch and feel the almost tangible yet somehow still elusive possibility and potential. As hard as we try, we remain incapacitated by soul ties that handicap our lives and prevent us from reaching our destiny. We are unable to ever "put our hands on it." We are unable to drive it home. No matter how many times we start the engine, we never get to experience the joy of the journey or the delight of the destination.

You see, we cannot receive what's behind that door if we're broken, fragmented, and tied to things that by their very nature are antagonistic to our success and our future. Sometimes God will close that door. He is a loving and responsible Father. He will not allow us to move into a destiny moment if we are unprepared or ill-prepared for what lies behind that door. He loves us too much and cares for our success too much to allow us to squander His best in our fragile and wounded condition. We must be healed!

HEALING IS A PROCESS

Although there are examples of instantaneous healing throughout Scripture, as well as experienced in some parts of the world today, sometimes healing is found in a *process*. As an example of this, let's consider a passage from the ninth chapter of John's gospel.

> *"As He passed by, He saw a man blind from birth. {2} And His disciples asked Him, 'Rabbi, who sinned, this man or his parents, that he would be born blind?' {3} Jesus answered, 'It was neither that this man sinned, nor his parents; but it was so that the works of God might be displayed in him. {4} I must work the works of Him who sent Me as long as it is day; night is coming when no one can work. {5} While I am in the world, I am the Light of the world.' {6} When He had said this, He spat on the ground, and made clay of the spittle, and applied the clay to his eyes, {7} and said to him, 'Go, wash in the pool of Siloam' (which is translated, Sent). So he went away and washed, and came back seeing."*

> **John 9:1-7**

> We can become so familiar with our impairment that what is, by God's standard, abnormal becomes our normal!

Here, Jesus encounters a man who has been blind from birth. One of the interesting things to note is that Jesus was passing by, so therefore, we can safely deduce that this man was stationary. No doubt he had been pretty much in the same place most of his life. It was familiar. It was even comfortable.

Do you realize that we can become comfortable with dysfunction? We can become so familiar with our impairment that what is, by God's standard, abnormal becomes our normal!

For Jesus to encounter blind people was nothing unusual. The crowds followed Him everywhere He went, and Jesus healed the blind, the deaf, and the mute as a matter of course. However, the actual miracle that Jesus did for this blind man was somewhat different, and apparently important enough to mention and be included as part of the Biblical account of Jesus' life. Something very significant took place here which is vital to us as we deal with soul ties.

For a moment, imagine that you are there with Jesus and the blind man. Light was all around this blind man, but he could not see it. The beauty of creation wasn't any less magnificent that day, even though he could not enjoy it, nor participate in it. The blind man was completely surrounded by light and was being engaged by *the* Light—naturally and spiritually—but yet, he lacked the ability to see it, obtain it, or comprehend it. Sound familiar?

What I want you to understand now is how Jesus set out a path—a process, if you will—for this man to receive his total healing. Obviously, He could have just spoken the word or laid His hands on the man, or even commanded the spirit of infirmity to leave him; it would have been done! But that's not what Jesus did!

Instead, He spits on the ground, mixes the spit with dirt, and forms a clay-like mud. Can't you just imagine what is going on in the blind man's head? While he is unable to see what is transpiring, his sense of hearing is very keen. He hears Jesus spit! Now, Jesus begins applying this spit-made mud to the man's eyes. No doubt at this moment everyone who is watching is shocked, amazed, and maybe even a little bit disgusted. It is, in fact, a humiliating process, nevertheless, one Jesus has chosen to use. Once He applies the concoction, Jesus commands the man to go and wash at the pool of Siloam.

"Siloam" means *sent*. Jesus required this man to leave the comfortable and the familiar and go to a place he did not know in order that he might be healed. The blind man had to participate in the process, even though he did not know what to expect. He had to be willing to change his position. He had to be willing to deal with humiliation, embarrassment, apprehension, shame, and perhaps a myriad of other emotions. The bottom line was this man had to walk it out.

Like this blind man, the time has come for us to begin to see what we could not see before. It's time for our blinded eyes to be opened to the things that are handicapping and limiting us. In order for that to happen, we must first acknowledge (that is, accept knowledge) the spiritual blindness in which we presently find ourselves. We must submit to the process of healing and complete restoration, thereby positioning ourselves to receive all of God's very best for our lives. We must choose to trust God with our lives, move out of our current debilitating mindset, and take this journey, knowing that God has our best interest in mind.

HERE'S THE DEAL

Going back to the "Let's Make a Deal" example I used earlier, imagine you're standing in front of the winning door right now. Behind that door is everything you have been believing God for; everything the Word of God promises you as a Believer—your dreams, your purpose, and your destiny. To attain it, you will be required to do some serious, honest soul-searching. You will have to ask yourself some difficult questions and answer them from your heart.

- ◆ Am I willing to lay my pride and religious mindset on the altar and press through to a complete and total breakthrough in my life?

- ◆ Can I be brutally honest with myself as I look at my past and present—the good, the bad, and the ugly?

- ◆ Am I willing to trust God with my life, my future, my heart?

- ◆ Am I willing to be obedient and do what is necessary to have the handicap removed, regain my eyesight, and experience genuine Kingdom living in every area of my life?

Your heart level answers to these questions will determine whether you will unlock the destiny God has for you. It is the choice between life and death.

"I call heaven and earth to witness against you today, that I have set before you life and death, the blessing and the curse. So choose life in order that you may live, you and your descendants."

Deuteronomy 30:19

There it is: death . . . life. God says, "Choose life!" Only you can make the decision to take the limits off of your life! Now is the time to start the process of healing, recovery, and restoration. Let's walk this out together. Let's see what God has in store for us.

CHAPTER 3

Created in His Image

Understanding Your Identity

You've heard it since you sat as a child in Sunday school class: You are created in God's image. Although you may have heard it taught and preached all of your life, it is possible that you still may not fully grasp the magnitude and importance of this truth. As a human being, you are the physical manifestation of God in the earth. But just what does that mean exactly? The entirety of this chapter is dedicated to teaching and showing you the manner in which God created you and who you really are in Him. It is only when you understand *how* you were created that you can begin to assess your weaknesses, insecurities, and—for the sake and purpose of this book—be able to recognize how soul ties operate in your life and where in your being they originate.

In the Beginning

Throughout Genesis Chapter 1 appears the phrase over and over again, ***"Then God said, 'Let there be . . .'"*** Every time God uttered a word out of His mouth, whatever it was that He said would literally—out of nothing and out of nowhere—become manifest in the earth. When God created Mankind, however, He took a completely different approach.

> ***"Then God said, 'Let Us make man in Our image, according to Our likeness; and let them rule over the fish of the sea and over the birds of the sky and over the cattle and over all the earth, and over every creeping thing that creeps on the earth.'"***
>
> **Genesis 1:26**

It's interesting that when it came time to create Man, the Bible doesn't say, "Then God said, 'Let *there be* man.'" The fact that Mankind is the only creation God did not ***speak*** into existence is what makes us so incredibly unique. Instead, God said, ***"Let us make man."***

God initiated a conversation with His complete being. "Let us…" Everything that was, was contained in Him. Out of His complexity and tripartite nature, He said, "Let Us, *in Our entirety*, make man in Our image, according to Our likeness." Let him *be like Us and look just like Us—a three-part being* (italics added)." While there is but one God, the fact is, God is not one-dimensional. He is at the very least three-dimensional. He is Father, Son, and Holy Spirit.

Using the model of Himself—a three-part being—He created an exact replica of His image in the earth. He was looking for an entity that could effectively, and with great efficiency, rule and reign over everything He had created. This being had to be in the same likeness and image of His being. Also, because God used His words to create the world and everything in it, this earthly representation of His being must not only *look like* God Himself, but also *carry the same authoritative, creative voice.* Creation would not know the difference. When the animals heard Man speak, they would literally hear the voice of the same One who said, "Let there be . . . ." But for Man to have this type of authority, he would first have to be **complete** in all areas. In the New Testament, the Apostle Paul addressed it in this way:

"Now may the God of peace Himself sanctify you entirely; and may your spirit and soul and body be preserved complete, without blame at the coming of our Lord Jesus Christ."

1 Thessalonians 5:23

Notice some key words in this passage. Paul's prayer is for us to be sanctified *entirely.* The King James Version uses the word *wholly* and the New King James Version uses the word *completely.* Then, Paul goes on to describe exactly what "entirely" entails: *our spirit, soul, and body.* If we, as Christians, are going to live the life God has designed for us, then we must be entirely complete, one hundred percent, with all three parts of our God-designed being functioning at full capacity and in perfect synchronicity.

All of creation is subservient to God because God Himself spoke it into existence. Think about this for a minute. The ultimate authority of any written book is who? The author. Why? Because he or she is the one who created it. The book originated in the mind of that person, and they formed the thought into a completed work. In comparison, the Bible says that Jesus is the *author* and the finisher of our faith (Hebrews 12:2). He created our faith, or as we sometimes call it, our belief system. One of the most important things of being created in God's image, according to Genesis 1:26, is that we are to have dominion over creation. In other words, we have the ability to use our voice, just as God used His voice, and direct creation as the Kingdom of God would mandate. This is a major factor in understanding and walking out the Kingdom life.

Although many people understand, in theory, the principles of living a Kingdom life, they cannot exercise or implement God's Kingdom on the earth mainly because their voice is distorted. Another way to think of it is this: what God desires to do in and through a person somehow gets "lost in transmission." Somewhere along the way, there has been a breakdown within the matrix of that person's spirit, soul, and body; therefore, when they speak God's Word, their voice becomes warbled and distorted and it carries no authoritative power. God's Word in creation carried power and results because *all* three parts of His being were in sync, in agreement with one another, and fully functional. If we are going to live as Kingdom people and be God's image on the earth, it is imperative that our whole being—spirit, soul, and body—be healthy, in agreement, in alignment, and working properly, according to the Designer's intentions. There is no other option!

THE SOUL OF MAN

One of the most important factors of identifying the soul ties that keep us from living God's abundant life for us on this earth is understanding exactly what role the soul plays in our lives and how it affects our ability to achieve God's design.

> Our soul is the part of us that contains our thoughts, memories, wounds, desires, and our will.

Our soul is the part of us that contains our thoughts, memories, wounds, desires, and our will. Just stop and think about how much of our soul—our thoughts, memories, will, wounds, desires—control our everyday life. It's unbelievably huge if you think about it! This is why the Bible is very specific about *how* we prosper and live a complete life. Our ability to prosper is directly proportionate to the health of our soul.

> *"Beloved, I pray that in all respects you may prosper and be in good health, just as your soul prospers."*
>
> **3 John 1:2**

The overall well-being of our lives is completely controlled by the health and wholeness of our soul.

THE SOUL IS IN CONTROL

Our Governing Entity. Every nation in the world is ruled by some form of governing headship. They may be either elected or appointed or even set up by some unorthodox manner, but they still carry many of the same responsibilities. These governing bodies control the flow of commerce, develop economic structure, establish laws for individuals and organizations, and set guidelines to ensure these laws are followed. In short, they set the standard of what is legal and acceptable for a particular society or nation and what is not.

> The overall well-being of our lives is completely controlled by the health and wholeness of our soul.

Look at how Merriam-Webster's Dictionary defines the word term "govern." It's very interesting!

(1.) "To exercise continuous sovereign authority over; especially: to control and direct the making and administration of policy in; to rule without sovereign power and usually without having the authority to determine basic policy, (2.) To control the speed of (as a machine) especially by automatic means, (3.) To control, direct, or strongly influence the actions and conduct of; to exert a determining or guiding influence in or over, (4.) To serve as a precedent or deciding principle for, (5.) To prevail or have decisive influence."[3]

---

[3] http://www.m-w.com/dictionary/govern

Webster also gives synonyms for "govern" as: "control," "manipulate," and "restrain."[4]

Wow! A governing entity has a tremendous amount of influence in every area of our lives. With that in mind, ask yourself these questions:

- What (or who) is controlling you?

- Are there any people, situations, memories, feelings, or forces manipulating your life?

- What things are restraining (or limiting) you, your family, your marriage, your church, or your business from being all that God promised and intended?

These are questions I am going to ask you to think about as we go further on through this book. We will discuss them more in later chapters. Now, let's get back to the role of governing entities.

Some nations and governments would refer to a governing office as the "seat of authority." In the United States, where I live, many of our states are divided into counties or parishes. In each county or parish, there is a city that has been designated as the "county seat." It is the place from which the government administers its will over that particular county and is the central hub of all governing activity.

Our soul functions in the exact same way concerning our three-part being. It is the governing "seat" of our lives. It is what sets the boundaries and limits that ultimately determine

---

[4] Ibid.

the parameters within which we are allowed to operate. It regulates our drive and achievement to the maximum level its present health and stability will allow. *As our soul is healthy, so are the remaining parts of our being.*

SLOW DOWN A LITTLE!

Growing up, my neighborhood friends and I were always looking for an opportunity to drive a vehicle; not just any vehicle, but something with a little speed and excitement to it. It was a theoretical "mark of maturity" for someone to actually get behind the wheel of a car and drive away at will—especially at a high rate of speed. We longed for the day.

One of the first opportunities we ever had to actually live out this dream was through one of our neighbors who owned a go-cart. Not only was it a model of freedom for us, but it looked like a race car, to boot. Even though it had a small horsepower engine, to my friends and me, it was like strapping into an Indy car and watching for the green flag. All that was missing were the television cameras and the crowd.

I'll never forget when it was finally my turn to get behind the wheel of this machine that to my friends and I was the embodiment of freedom. As I strapped into the seat, I'm sure our neighbor's father was giving me some very important operational instructions and much needed safety tips. All I heard was, "Gentlemen, start your engines!" As soon as I was given the "green light," I was off to the races. The freedom! The rush! The thunder (or putter, rather) of the engine! The speed! But then, something very disconcerting began to happen.

46

Even though my foot was pushing the gas pedal all the way down to the floor, the go-cart reached its top speed—which in my estimation wasn't nearly as fast as it should be—and stopped accelerating. Very frustrated, I asked myself, "What's wrong with this thing? Why won't it go any faster? I've got the pedal down all the way!" Little did I know, my neighbor's father was a bit smarter than we were. Before he allowed his son—or for that matter, any of his friends—to drive, he installed a device that would not allow the go-cart to travel any faster than a predetermined speed. This clever device was called a *governor*. Its job was to regulate and control our speed while driving. No matter what we had imagined or dreamed, we could only go as fast as the governor would allow. It was an imposed ceiling to the potential of the machine.

Do you see the picture here? *Our soul is the governor of our lives!!* Not only does it control how we deal with the affairs of life and the decisions we make, it also is the key factor in how far we will go in life. It is the regulator of our dreams and possibilities. An unhealthy soul plagued by ungodly soul ties has the power to stop you dead in your tracks and never allow you to reach your full potential. Memories of failure, disappointments, wrecked relationships, losses, and wounds

> An unhealthy soul plagued by ungodly soul ties has the power to stop you dead in your tracks and never allow you to reach your full potential.

will take your dreams and visions and relegate you to a life of more set-backs, more lost opportunity, and eventually robs you of your hope.

Our job, as we go through this process together, is to identify and remove the limitations that have been regulating, governing, and detrimentally affecting our ability to have God's plan and destiny fulfilled in our lives. Let's move forward now, with this goal in mind.

CHAPTER 4

Understanding the Soul

The creation of Man was the first example of how God would duplicate His tripartite being here on the earth, but it is not the only pattern we see. Parallels of the tripartite nature of the Creator are witnessed throughout creation, illustrated throughout Scripture, and experienced in the Kingdom life, as well as everyday life. The way these many parallels are arranged, function, and operate is exactly modeled after how we were created in God's image. In this chapter, I want to provide you an in-depth understanding of the soul, and how it relates with the spirit and the body. As we go forward, you will begin to see how this part of our being affects every part of our life.

We have already established that Man was created just like God—in His image and in His likeness. An examination of the makeup of Mankind, or how we were created, has revealed that we are three-part beings. Just as God is Father, Son, and Holy Spirit, we were created with a spirit, a soul, and a body. It is imperative, according to Scripture, that we be whole, complete, and entirely together if we are to experience success and blessing. Every part of you is dependent on your soul for success, health, and fulfillment. As your soul goes, so goes your life.

Another important thing that we must establish is that there is an order by which our life is to operate as it relates to these three parts. The order that God intended is: **spirit, soul, body**—in that sequence. With that in mind, let's go a step further to see how these pieces work and operate together.

SPIRIT

The spirit of Man is that part of us that was created first, and can be referred to as the headship or ruling element in Man. "Headship" can be defined as a *God-designed system or function whereby divine order and structure can be administered so that the will and purpose of God may be facilitated and accomplished at its intended level.*

> Before we were a body or possessed a soul, we were created as a spirit being, just as God is a spirit.

With this understanding, it is easy to see why our spirit is designed to function as the headship element of our triune nature. It is because this is the part of Man that was cut directly out of God. Again, let me emphasize this one important point: before we were a body or possessed a soul, we were created as a spirit being, just as God is a spirit. Our spirit, as headship, provides us with some very important things.

50

Divine Connection. First and foremost, our spirit provides us connectivity to God. It is the only part of our being that grants us direct access to our heavenly Father. Through our spirits, we are supernaturally connected. We are interrelated with Him with no separation between us. Our spirits are just as much God as God is Himself. The very fact that we are cut out of God as a spirit makes us part of God and Him part of us.

Although we were created as spirit beings with direct access to God, that access was closed when Man willfully broke communion with the Father through original sin in the Garden of Eden. When we are born again, our spirit comes into alignment with God and that line of communication and access is reopened. That is why a Believer's prayer life is immensely important. We have a powerful privilege, and that is to have divine communication with the Creator of all things.

The very fact that Mankind is the only entity in God's creation that actually possesses a spirit proves that our connection is divine and is intended to communicate with our Creator. Nothing created before or after Man was made in the image and likeness of God.

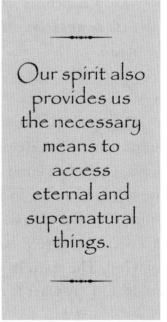

Our spirit also provides us the necessary means to access eternal and supernatural things.

Supernatural Access. Our spirit also provides us the necessary means to access eternal and supernatural things. If we begin to operate our lives under a different headship—

something other than our spirit—then we lose our keys to the eternal, supernatural dimension.

We have often said, "God and God alone has access to the eternal things of life." In one sense of the word, that is a correct statement. However, the God that is in us, or our spirit being, has the same access *as long as our spirit is in its proper position or relationship to God.* This is exactly why Jesus told us to pray, *"Thy kingdom come, Thy will be done in earth as it is in heaven,"* (Matthew 6:10, KJV). We can choose to recite this scripture as a writ or see it as ritual, but it will have no effect in our lives unless our spirit is operating in its proper order and alignment. To gain heavenly access and actually live the Kingdom life on this earth, our spirits *must* be in control of our lives. There is a great example of this principle found in the book of Matthew.

> *"Keep watching and praying that you may not enter into temptation; the spirit is willing, but the flesh is weak."*

> **Matthew 26:41**

Our spirit man knows what we should be doing in life. Our spirit knows the disciplines we should be activating on a daily basis. Our spirit knows, and consequently, speaks to us when we are functioning in a way that is not pleasing to God. Our spirit is constantly talking. It has the desire to be and act just like God because it is made in the exact image and likeness of God. The spirit is willing to withstand temptation; willing to do and say what is right; willing to make the sacrifices and changes to be and respond like God; willing to change and adjust for the sake of accomplishing the purposes of God.

If all of this is true—and it is—why, then, are there so many instances when our bodies and minds do things that are not God-like? Why are temptations constantly bombarding and taunting us? Why aren't we able to manifest the things our spirits so desperately desire? Why do we fall into some of the same traps over and over again? Why are we unable to manifest in the natural that God-likeness our spirit man so fervently aspires to achieve?

The reason is actually very simple. It is an indication that our spirit is not in control of our lives. We are being *governed* by a part of our being that was never intended to be in control. Remember, the spirit is willing, but the flesh is weak.

Let me describe it in these terms: your spirit desires to be everything God created you to be. Your spirit is intent on seeing the will of God come to fullness in your life; however, your flesh continues to manifest the opposite of—or at the very least, a limited version of—the complete plan of God. The flesh is not translating into reality what is being generated out of the heavens. Why? The answer lies, once again, in how we were created.

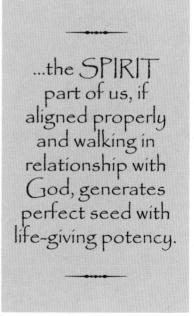

...the SPIRIT part of us, if aligned properly and walking in relationship with God, generates perfect seed with life-giving potency.

We are spirit, soul, and body. What is the connection between the spirit and the flesh? It is the soul! The condition of the soul is short-circuiting the results desired by the spirit from being manifest in our bodies. Let's explore now how this relationship works.

Seed-Carrying Agent. The spirit, being the rightful and legitimate headship of our life, is also the male gender part—or the seed-carrying agent—of our created being. The seed that is produced by the spirit, which is God in us, is faultless. It is perfect and it is pure. There are no discrepancies with the seed. Consider that in a perfect scenario (as I present in this case), when a male's seed is transferred, it carries enough power and potency to inseminate an egg and cause life to be generated. The seeds are perfect, just as the spirit part of our being has a perfect, Godly seed. In other words, the SPIRIT part of us, if aligned properly and walking in relationship with God, generates perfect seed with life-giving potency. So I submit that the spirit is the male, or seed-bearing agent, in our lives. The spirit is willing!

The soul is the place where memories are kept—good and bad. It is the place where wounds, hurts, disappointments, fears, and our sense of failures are contained.

THE SOUL

The next dimension of our creation—and the part this book is dedicated to—is our soul. *Our soul is the part of us that contains our will, our emotions, and our thoughts, which in turn, control the course of our mind and eventually produce our actions.* Everything that takes place in our mind is housed within the soulish arena of our created being. The soul is the place where memories are kept—good and bad. It is the place where wounds, hurts, disappointments, fears, and our sense of failures are contained.

Even though these emotions and feelings are real—and we *all* have them—they cannot be released or activated by themselves. They require an activator, or in other words, a seed; thus, our soul is the female part of our created being. It is *the womb* of man. Let me reiterate that when God created man in His own image and likeness, He created *both male and female* but only formed one body and breathed both into man. When God decided to give man another perspective, which is woman, He went physically inside man and took a part of man's internal anatomy and used it to frame the foundational building blocks of the woman.

Have you ever wondered where the word "woman" comes from? It comes from the root word, "womb." Womb-man translates into woman. Before the woman was taken out of Adam, his body contained the womb. Therefore, the physical being later called "woman" was actually the extracted womb that came out of God's initial creation, Adam, which was created in His image to begin with. It was the "womb-man," or woman, walking in the earth.

The soul is the womb of our created being. It is the female agency, capable of receiving and carrying seed. Remember I mentioned earlier that our spirit, which is connected to God, is the male, seed-carrying element of our being. We know now that our soul is the entity within which the seed connects, insemi-nates, conceives, and creates life. Understanding the two roles and characteristics of these two parts of our being, it is easy to see why our spirit (or seed) is willing, but our flesh cannot pro-duce what our seed intends. It is because the soul (or womb) is incapable of adequately carrying and nurturing the seed.

GATEWAYS THROUGH THE SOUL

One of the most powerful truths a Spirit-filled Christian can ever learn is this: a regenerated spirit cannot be demon-pos-sessed. Satan cannot degrade or affect your spirit because it is God's. He has no authority in the spirit dimension of your life. Understand, however, that every Christian will at some time or another experience an attack of demonic activity which can lead to oppression, depression, physical sickness, or many other symptoms. However, the only access Satan and demonic influ-ences have to your spirit life is *through your soul*—your thoughts, beliefs, hurts, wounds, unre-solved issues, ungodly soul ties, and curses. This is the crack in

> ...the only access Satan and demonic influences have to your spirit life is through your soul—your thoughts, beliefs, hurts, wounds, unresolved issues, ungodly soul ties, and curses.

the door and the only entrance by which we can be penetrated and affected by demonic activity.

Now, can you see why our souls are so important to our physical, spiritual, and emotional health? Is it any wonder why the devil would constantly be attacking this part of our being?

Our soul can be the very agent that releases us into full prosperity of life or the prison that never allows us to grow past our mistakes. It can guide us or destroy us. The soulish area is where your beliefs are; what you actually believe about God, yourself, and the things and people around you. The Bible is very clear on how our soul—that is, our thinking—controls our lives.

"For as a man thinks in his heart, so is he . . ."

Proverbs 23:7

Where is the emotional heart of Man? In the soul. This is not about "mind over matter." If this concept were true, then your "matter" wouldn't matter any more! You would just exercise your mind and everything would be alright. The truth is, it's your "matter" that is sabotaging your life, and your mind does not have the capacity to take control. There is no mystical way to think

What my life produces in the natural is a direct result and outcome of what my spirit and soul have conceived and given birth to.

your way out of your current situations. Instead, you have to learn how to rule your soul and the patterns that govern your life.

THE BODY

The third part of our tri-natured being is the body, which is our created physical being with its health and wellness, or lack thereof. Our body is also the tangible representation and expressed reality of our appetites, cravings, and lifestyle, and displays the outcome of what we put our minds to and accomplish in life. Our physical body is how our three-part being manifests in the earth realm.

When my spirit (the seed-carrier) inseminates my soul (the womb), my body will always manifest whatever the soul is capable of producing. The body, then, symbolizes the offspring of my tripartite being. What my life produces in the natural is a direct result and outcome of what my spirit and soul have conceived and given birth to.

The Perfect Seed. In the beginning of this chapter, I made mention of the male seed being perfect. Obviously, in the physical realm, this is not always the case; but let's consider how this relates to our spirit being.

Your spirit is the perfect seed from God. It is the only piece of your tri-natured being that is perfectly connected to God Himself. To someone who has received a regenerated spirit, or has been born again (see John Chapter 3), the seed, or the renewed spirit, cannot be contaminated! The God in you is *perfect*. The God in you cannot make a wrong decision. Your spirit which is connected directly to God is absolutely flawless. It is very easy to see that most of our "spiritual problems" are actually not spiritual at all. This would implicate your seed, or spirit, as being the one creating all of the havoc and disarray in your life. But the issue is not with the seed; the problem lies within the womb—or the soul.

The spirit of man is God's perfect seed. For the soul to be perfected, it is necessary that it be inseminated with the seed, which is God's Word. The Bible tells us about the parable of the sower in three of the four Gospels (Matthew 13:3-8, Mark 4:3-20, and Luke 8:5-8). When God spoke His word in eternity, it went forth as a seed, which He intended to see manifest in time. According to the pattern of all things, it would be necessary that the Word, being seed, be planted in a womb; which, in the case of humanity, would mean in our *souls*.

I believe that God is still very actively speaking in the earth today. Through the years, I have seen many people receive a prophetic word from the Lord. They were very quick to share that God was "going to do" this and they were "going to do" that, or that God had promised to bring such-and-such about in their lives. Their goals were honorable and admirable: to see ministries birthed, to have their quality of life progress, and to walk in prosperity and blessing. However, when it came time to "give birth" to this seed (or offspring), the results were far from what they had originally imagined, dreamed of, and hoped for. Their belief was correct, their confession was in agreement with the Word, and their expectations were high; but something was not functioning properly within them. The

Word (the perfect seed) was planted and the outcome (off-spring) could be seen *by faith*; but there was a major break-down in the *womb* (the soul), thus causing the final product to be non-existent or essentially deformed.

Three Possible Results. In the physical realm, when a womb is impregnated, there are three different results that can occur.

1. Miscarriage

   Practically every woman who becomes pregnant has to, at some point, work through the thought of the possibility of having a miscarriage. It is really not a fear, but rather a concern that is natu-ral for most women. Essentially, she wonders if her body will be strong enough to produce life, and if her womb will be healthy enough to sustain life through the gestation process.

2. Abortion

   It would be completely incredulous to say that every woman who is pregnant contemplates abortion. That simply is not the case. The fact is, however, many pregnancies are never carried to full-term or delivery. Whether by choice or because of medical reasons, outside forces can sometimes cause the fetus or child to be removed from the womb, ter-minating and prematurely ending the natural cycle of pregnancy.

3. Birth

> One of the most extraordinary experiences of life is the birth of a baby and bringing a new life into the world. Personally, for my wife and I, two of the greatest days of our lives were when we gave birth to our two children, Christian and Abigail. If you have children of your own, you can relate to this feeling. There's nothing like it in the world.

During conception, the woman's womb receives the male seed and becomes pregnant. The seed is then carried, developed, nurtured, and eventually delivered and brought into the world as a physical new life, a newborn baby.

Sadly, not all pregnancies end in this blissful joy. In some cases, even when a pregnancy is carried full-term and delivered, the newborn baby is not always "perfect," or what was envisioned by the mother and father. Problems can arise during the term of pregnancy that can cause some babies to be born prematurely. Still, others may be born with physical deformities or mental deficiencies or other types of challenges. An even more severe and frightening result of birth is when a baby is delivered, but is stillborn. This is a medical term for a baby that is born dead. In the case of a stillborn baby, even though the physical body of the baby was delivered, he or she never experienced life on this earth.

It's in the Womb

One of the many reasons for these negative conclusions to pregnancy is attributed to the woman's womb not having the capacity to carry or properly protect and nurture the seed that has been implanted. These three outcomes of insemination are not only evident in the natural pregnancy process, but they are very real concerning our lives and our destinies, as well.

OUR DNA

In the natural realm, children are conceived, developed, and born with several distinctive factors. For example, they carry the DNA and genetic codes of their mother and father. These generational, genetic strands provide a predisposition to certain health issues, disease characteristics, physical traits, similarities, deformities, personality strengths and weaknesses, motivations, and individual desires and affections.

There is a spiritual parallel to this natural truth. While each of us possesses DNA in our natural being, we also have various spiritual qualities, predispositions, and patterns handed down to us through generational transfer. We are born with these. They are inherent within us and affect our lives, with or without our permission. For some, these may include particular strengths, blessings, or talents; while others find themselves struggling with weaknesses, iniquitous patterns, curses, and pain. Each of us deal with the DNA factor, naturally and spiritually, and must be reconciled to God so that we can experience the full measure of His intent for us.

> *"Therefore, if anyone is in Christ he is a new creature; the old things passed away; behold, new things have come. Now all these things are from God, who reconciled Himself through Christ, and gave us the*

ministry of reconciliation, namely, that God was in Christ reconciling the world to Himself, not counting their trespasses against them, and He has committed to us the word of reconciliation."

2 Corinthians 5:17-18

Our spirit was created from God's Spirit. Our spirit contains DNA from the seed of God's Word, which is infallible and incorruptible. Nevertheless, if we continue to live with a wounded, damaged, or sick soul—or womb—we will never be able to conceive and/or properly give birth to or produce healthy "offspring"—thereby manifesting the things God has said about us, given us by inheritance, and promised to us in His Word.

We have to recognize and deal with the inherited DNA that resides in our soul—generational curses, rejection from previous relationships, abandonment, unforgiveness, depression, self-esteem issues. The list goes on and on. These issues, and more, are preventing us from carrying the seed full-term and experiencing a healthy delivery!

There have been countless people throughout time who carried God's seed of promise: a thriving business, a completely healthy body, a marriage that is in total harmony and union, children who are complete and whole, ministries fully functioning to affect and change the world for the Kingdom. All these promises were deposited into their spirit; however, the offspring from a wounded, unhealthy, or dysfunctional soul (womb) will either be:

1. Miscarried

   If we cannot properly nourish God's seed for continued growth and development, it never has a chance for sustained life. God's promises for us are rejected by our soul and die in the formation stage.

2. Aborted

   Our soulish arena, or mindset, cannot understand the magnitude of what God has promised for us. Because we have previously tried and failed, we make the decision—consciously or unconsciously—to end the process rather than to endure the pain and discomfort of the development and birthing process.

3. Birthed, but with Defects

   The dream is birthed, but it is not all God intended it to be. The womb did not have the capacity to fully develop the seed.

Far too many people in the Church today are constantly asking themselves, "God, why don't you do this?" or "When is this going to manifest in my life?" or even, "Why does everything in my life seem to turn out all wrong?" You can watch their life over the course of ten, fifteen, or even twenty years, and it is the same cycle over, and over, and over again. They always seem to wind up back at ground zero and starting all over on their journey. I can speak from experience: this type of life is completely unfulfilling! You can carry the most powerful and authentic gift from God, and still live on this seemingly never-ending merry-go-round. "But I'm a child of God. I'm a Believer," you say. So, what happened? Did God lie? Did He change His mind about you midstream? Did He stretch the truth a little? Dangle a carrot in front of you?

NO! Absolutely not! He cannot lie if He wanted to.

"God is not a man, that He should lie, nor a son of man, that He should repent; Has He said, and will He not do it? Or has He spoken, and will He not make it good?"

Numbers 23:19

He did not lie, nor did He mislead you, or say something on accident. He meant what He said and said what He meant. *The seed is perfect. It's from God and God is perfect!* The problem is not the seed; it is the womb.

THERE IS GREAT NEWS!

Spiritually speaking, whenever you abort, miscarry, and/or deliver an imperfect baby from God's seed, He does not cause you to have to be impregnated all over again! You are still carrying the seed. God simply begins the whole process *in you* all over again.

Just as the beginning stages of a natural pregnancy can cause symptoms of nausea, dizziness, and an overall feeling of queasiness, so it is with the spiritual seed. You can, at times, feel very uncomfortable, even sick. But hang in there! The seed is once again beginning to develop in you and will eventually produce the will of God and His good pleasure for your life!

" . . . For it is God who is at work in you, both to will and to work for His good pleasure."

Philippians 2:13

Today, more than at any time in the history of Mankind, the Body of Christ is going through a restoration and healing of the womb, **the soul**. God is addressing many issues that have made our souls deficient, inadequate—or even worse— barren. We are beginning to understand that God's perfect will for our lives is that we function the way we were created: in HIS image and likeness.

Now, we must prepare the womb of our soul in order to carry His promises to full fruition in our lives. The "good work" God began in us now has the opportunity to become "completed until the day of Christ Jesus."

"For I am confident of this very thing, that He who began a good work in you will perfect it until the day of Christ Jesus."

Philippians 1:6

IT'S A DONE DEAL!

The same pattern is true with your tri-part being. Your spirit is connected to God and has a complete comprehension and retention of every single thing God has ever said about you or over you. He has scripted your life: every moment; every detail. Everything He intends to see manifest in your life is written from before the foundations of the world. He is the Alpha and Omega and knows the beginning and the end (Revelation 21:6).

"Before I formed you in the womb I knew you, and before you were born, I consecrated you . . ."

Jeremiah 1:5

In the moment of redemptive manifestation on the cross, Jesus said, "It is finished," (John 19:30). This was not a final announcement of, "Okay, I'm done now." No, no, no! Jesus was declaring something much more powerful. "IT"—everything God has ever said, planned, and designed—was now totally restored back to Mankind. The work of restoration was finished, done, and completed for all humanity; once and for all. Once again, Man would be able to live the life God had originally intended—a life created in His image and in His likeness!

So, where does the short circuit take place? Why is the perfect seed in our spirit producing such dysfunctional and lackluster offspring? Again, it is in the soul. Remember, the spirit (seed) is willing, but the flesh (soul) is weak. Our wounds, hurts, and even things deeply imbedded in our subconscious—things we cannot consciously remember—keep us from experiencing what God "finished" at the cross. There could even be generational issues going back as far as five and six, maybe even ten generations that are still affecting your soulish arena. You might not even be aware of their origin, but their consequences are evident in your everyday life. As with Creation itself, our entire being has to be properly aligned for us to function as we were created. We must allow our spirit to become the dominant and controlling agency, so that our soul, or womb, can begin to produce the desired offspring in our lives.

> We must allow our spirit to become the dominant and controlling agency, so that our soul, or womb, can begin to produce the desired offspring in our lives.

FRAGMENTED LIVES

All three parts of our created being must be functioning holistically, together, in order. If one part is out of sorts, it is going to affect the other two. That's just the way it works. It is the way God designed us to be. If we want to function in wholeness, we have to deal with our total being. We cannot address spiritual issues and ignore the soul; it does not work.

Consider this: when a person's body is in relationship with God, we say that person is "healthy." Likewise, when a person's spirit is in relationship with God, we say they are "holy." And what about their soul? When it is in relationship with God, then they are "happy." Too many times, people are living with only two-thirds of this equation functioning well. There is a missing piece. They are healthy and holy, but are never happy. They love God. They serve, they pray, and they believe God's Word, but never seem to have inner peace or any consistent growth and progress in life. Why is this? Their soul is not well.

The same is true for those who battle long-term and major illnesses. Think about that for just a minute. There are Believers everywhere who are spiritually and mentally healthy, but their bodies are sick and diseased. They have battled illnesses and physical challenges all their lives; yet they continue to live happy and content. Their soul is well, their spirit is in line; but their body falls short of what God desires for them. Again, they are missing the wholeness of life.

> *"Beloved, I pray that in all respects you may prosper and be in good health, just as your soul prospers."*
>
> **3 John 2**

This scripture specifically deals with the relationship between all three parts of our being:

Spirit — ". . . that you may prosper . . ."

Body — ". . . and be in good health . . ."

Soul — ". . . just as your soul prospers."

So many Believers struggle in one or more of these areas due to an unrecognized and/or unresolved soul tie. Understand this, the effects of *soul ties are not just limited to the "soulish" part of your being.* They definitely can, and do, affect your spirit and body as well. When soul ties are not recognized, or they are ignored and not dealt with, they will eventually begin to affect your whole being. Soul ties know no boundaries and will eventually work to destroy your entire life!

THE RIGHT COMBINATION

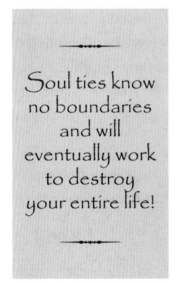

Soul ties know no boundaries and will eventually work to destroy your entire life!

When all three parts of our being are functioning in harmony and completeness, the results are wonderful. Our lives are whole. There are no missing pieces or dysfunctional parts. The Bible describes this life as one full of righteousness, peace, and joy. It is the way God made us to be, and is paramount to the Kingdom philosophy of life.

This book is dedicated to revealing the origin, condition, weaknesses, and the healing process of the soul. When our soul is restored and whole, then and only then, will we have the capacity to fully contain all of God's best that He has preordained for our lives!

"For the kingdom of God is not meat and drink; but righteousness, and peace, and joy in the Holy Ghost."

Romans 14:17 (KJV)

When a person finds himself or herself in the state of being "complete"—spirit, soul, and body—they will begin to experience the fullness of this scripture. Since we know that God is a just God (Deuteronomy 32:4), then we also know that He would not give us the pattern for a Kingdom life without providing us with the necessary tools to achieve it. Right?

Well, of course not. God is the one Who designed this life of wholeness. It is called being "created in His image." Jesus died a brutal death and gave His very life to purchase our right to have this life, to live in it, and to experience it to its fullness. Now, are you willing to allow the Holy Spirit to reveal the obstacles that need to be removed for you to walk in the wholeness of life? To live in the image of God as you were created? Your answer determines your completeness. Let's walk it out, together!

Section II

—

Indicators or
Effects
of
Soul Ties

CHAPTER 5

Soul Ties

You now have the foundation necessary to begin the process of understanding how soul ties work, what their affects are on our lives, and how to deal with them once we recognize them operating in our lives.

WHAT IS A SOUL TIE?

A soul tie occurs when the emotions, the mind and the will of a person becomes entangled to the point where their thoughts are no longer their own. They can no longer operate independently of somebody or something else. It is when a person or an entity is unnaturally and/or inordinately affected by the will, the emotions, the desires, or the situations of another. The secular world (clinical psychologists and the medical community) recognizes this basic issue in several ways, one of which is a condition they have labeled "codependency."[5] Numerous books and papers have been written dealing with

---

[5] A psychological condition or a relationship in which a person is controlled or manipulated by another who is affected with a pathological condition (as an addiction to alcohol or heroin); broadly : dependence on the needs of or control by another; http://www.m-w.com/dictionary/codependency

the study and treatment of codependency. So many have been diagnosed as being codependent and have only been treated according to the symptoms of what the condition was producing at the moment. Unfortunately, classical methods of dealing with this issue seldom ever resolve the person's symptoms, much less the root issues. Why? Because when we only deal with symptomatic treatment, we are not reaching the real cause. By not getting to the root of their problems, at best, we are placing a bandage on an arterial hemorrhage. In order to truly heal the person, we must first heal the soul! When a soul tie is present, then you must know that your soul is united with those people or things with which you have the soul tie. Whatever is going on in their lives will also affect you. Soul ties bind us—or tie us—to a person's weaknesses, curses, traumas, emotions, pain, and limitations. Soul ties will allow us to succeed to a certain point in our life, but never beyond a certain point—ever. There is an unseen ceiling on our progress or success. We wonder why we can never break through to the next level or into the next step. It is because we are anchored to something that is ungodly and unwholesome as it relates to our God-given destiny. Soul ties and certain covenants we make in life can cause us to be limited and restricted in the pursuit of our purpose, our dreams, our goals, and the plans of God for our lives.

> Soul ties will allow us to succeed to a certain point in our life, but never beyond a certain point—ever.

Here's a perfect example of how a soul tie operates. There is a huge, outdoor, inflatable game you can rent for events and parties. The game has two lanes with a wall in between them. They strap a harness and a belt around you and an identical harness and belt around another person. It's a race and the object is to see who can be the first to grab a Styrofoam ball attached by Velcro at the end of the wall that is dividing your lanes. Here's the catch, though: there is a bungee cord attached to both of your backs. As hard as you try to run forward, the bungee cord is pulling against you. It always seems to snap you backwards, slamming your body down to the floor where you started the whole process. By about the fourth or fifth try, you're completely out of breath, out of energy, worn-out, and for some of us, in serious need of medical attention!

As you look up, you see the Styrofoam ball (the goal) still in its place, out of your reach, untouched, and unattained. You keep thinking, "Just one more time. It's not *that* far. How hard can this be? Come on! Just run harder and reach out and grab it!" Again and again, the same results.

Like our efforts are on the inflatable game, our desire is sincere; our commitment is unfailing; we have the will. We're doing all the right things; we're giving our best effort, to the degree of wearing ourselves out trying. We have to become free *and* whole—*body, soul, and spirit*—if we are going to go where God wants us to go. Just like that bungee cord that kept us from moving forward and wore us out, we cannot afford to have soul ties attached to our lives that continue to hold us back from God's designed destiny and purpose in our life. Again:

"Beloved, I pray that in all respects you may prosper and be in good health, just as your soul prospers."

3 John 1:2

Let me paraphrase this verse: *If your soul is in a healthy place; (untied, unrestricted and unhindered by anything that is ungodly or unhealthy from the past), then you will experience the fullness of God's intent, which is good health and true prosperity.* I cannot stress to you enough that our ability to be prosperous, healthy, and complete in life is completely contingent upon and directly proportionate to how healthy our soul is. If we have unhealthy and ungodly soul ties in our life, they will affect every area of our life.

> The problem is not our desire; it is the limitations that have been invisibly and consistently keeping us from obtaining what we want and what God wants for us.

THE CYCLE

Soul ties always operate in cyclical patterns. You may function for years at a time and things seem to be doing well, but in seasons, the bottom drops out. There are some tell-tale signs to watch for. As you read the following pages, examine yourself to see if any of these patterns or statements apply to you, or even to someone that you love.

♦ Living the rollercoaster life: up-down-up-down-up-down

78

- High highs, low lows

- Feeling scattered and unclear in your mind

FINANCES

- Struggling financially all the time

- Can't break the cycle of living paycheck to paycheck

- Extra money comes in (i.e., tax refund) only to have an "unexpected" emergency or need arise (i.e., a trip to the doctor, car breaks down, air conditioner or heater goes out in your house, you or a child get sick and have to miss work)

- Always passed up on promotions

- Still too many bills left after your paycheck is long gone

- Have trouble envisioning yourself out of debt

- Always miss good opportunities to make money or miss good investment opportunities

- Business or investment opportunities always seem to be "a day late and a dollar short"

- Can never save money

RELATIONSHIPS

- Can never seem to maintain or retain healthy relationships

- Always lonely

- Feel abandoned and forgotten

- Always feel taken advantage of and used

- Find it difficult to receive love and affection

- "Can't trust anyone; they will hurt me"

EMOTIONS

- Hot tempered – always angry

- Never able to laugh and feel joy

- Suffer with depression and anxiety

- Fear of failure

- Poor self-image and self-esteem

- Always beating yourself up

- No confidence – do not believe in yourself

PHYSICAL HEALTH

- Always sick

- Never feel good

- Have no energy and strength

- Always feel burned-out and finished

- Overweight and unhealthy

Do these statements or situations sound familiar—too familiar?

See Jane Flip-Flop

Allow me to introduce "Jane" to you. She's the typical thirty-something individual. When I ask her how she's doing, one week she says, "Everything's great!" The next week, "Life just stinks!" The next week, "I'm doing wonderful! Couldn't be better!" The next week, "Oh, I'm okay. Life's just hard sometimes. I'll get through it." The next week: "Awesome!"

Can you see the pattern here?

Do you know this person?

Maybe you *are* this person?

Do you find yourself on a rollercoaster of cyclical patterns of extreme highs and even lower lows? You find yourself in up-and-down cycles of doing great, doing bad, doing great, doing bad, doing great. Why is this? It is because when you are not doing well, and going through various trials or struggles, you will tend to stand on the Word and believe God to sustain you and bring you through that season. Once in the clear, you do great for a while; but that is only short-lived because eventually, you hit a ceiling—the actual limitation that the soul tie or belief has created for you.

Inside-Out vs. Outside-In Living

We already know our soul contains the thoughts, the memories, the will, and the intellect of our being. Again, according to 3 John 2, we know that in order for every area of our life to prosper, our soul has to be healthy and free. This is what I call "inside-out living." Our world has taught us that we have to treat the outward and allow it to go inward; but the fact of the matter is, Scripture tells us that we are supposed to live inside-out, rather than outside-in. If the inside is prospering and healthy, everything on the outside will manifest accordingly.

Jesus said it this way in Matthew 23:25-27:

"Woe to you, scribes and Pharisees, hypocrites! For you clean the outside of the cup and of the dish, but inside they are full of robbery and self-indulgence. You blind Pharisee, first clean the inside of the cup and of the dish, so that the outside may become clean also. Woe to you, scribes and Pharisees, hypocrites! For you are like whitewashed tombs which on the outside appear beautiful, but inside they are full of dead men's bones and all uncleanness."

Wow! I believe Jesus was intent on making this point. It is time for the people of God to stop working so hard to project the "image" that we have it all together, and begin focusing on that part of us that really matters: the *inside*. When we begin to get the soul healed and set free, then everything in our lives begins to manifest the goodness and greatness of God in us.

We are moving forward into deeper areas of reflection. Open your heart. Allow the Holy Spirit to speak to you.

Are you tired of the same old thing happening over and over? Are you ready to move beyond the limitations that have you stuck in this demoralizing cycle of life? Will you go deeper with me now? Let's see what God has for you as we continue this journey.

CHAPTER 6

Behavioral Signs

Are there soul ties in effect and operating in your life? Would you even realize if they were? While you're reading over the next few pages, I want you to clear from your mind any and all preconceived ideas, all religious mindsets, and any thoughts or notions that would cause you to excuse away symptoms of ungodly soul ties by saying, "Well, that's just how I am," or "Well, that's just my personality."

This entire chapter is dedicated to bringing to light and assessing soul ties that could be operating in your life. Remember, before we can rid our lives of soul ties, we must first recognize them so we can aggressively deal with them. Then, and only then, will we be free to be who God made us to be and be able to walk in the abundance and the fulfillment of the Kingdom life God has promised us in His Word.

Behavioral Signs of a Soul Tie

These behavioral signs discussed below are classic indicators that soul ties are in operation in our lives. As you read through these, take time to make written notes of anything the Holy Spirit may bring to your mind.

1. **Irrational thinking**

   An ungodly soul tie will produce irrational thinking. "Irrational thinking" is defined as, *"thinking that does not follow a form or a measure of good sense or sensibility, or discernment."* It is where you make decisions out of a reactionary mode, as opposed to reason and controlled thought. You *react* as opposed to *acting*. Believe me when I say there is a great difference.

2. **Evaluating and levying judgments based on previous experiences**

   When we evaluate or judge our life and others according to something that happened to us in the past, there is reason to suspect a soul tie. This one is so important. It is almost like we are looking through a set of glasses that makes us see things different than reality. It causes us to live in a pseudo-reality—the prefix "pseudo-" meaning *false*. We develop a mind-set, or a pattern of thinking, which makes us see ourselves, other people, situations, or events based on something that happened to us previously. It could be something that happened a long time ago or something that happened last week. We are dealing with a reality that exists only because of a soul tie and not based on the truth of what God's intent and will for our life is today.

3. Emotionally dead

This is a strong indicator of the presence of a soul tie. It can also be a dangerous sign, if not recognized. They are unable to give or receive or interact emotionally with others. They often feel lifeless and dead on the inside. Slowly, they begin to pull away from life and isolate themselves from family and friends, gravitating to a world all of their own.

> A soul tie always causes an individual to shut themselves down emotionally in a particular area of their heart and mind.

4. Fantasy

In addition, when an individual shuts down emotionally, it usually means they are not capable of dealing with reality. Many times, they will tend to engage in what I will call, "fantasy living." I realize when most people hear the word "fantasy," they automatically think of it as having a sexual connotation. Sexual fantasies are a big part of it, and we will address that in a later chapter; but to limit it to just that leaves out many other issues that are just as important and concerning.

The word "fantasy" actually comes from the Middle English word "fancy." To "fantasize" is defined as *to portray in the mind*. An older spelling of the word fantasy is "phantasy," which also comes from the same root word where we get "phantom." Interestingly enough, the word "phantom" means *something apparent to sense but with no substantial existence*.

A person can engage in fantasy through a variety of outlets. Listed below are a few of common ones.

Prescription And Non-Prescription Drugs: One might begin to abuse prescription and non-prescription drugs such as sedatives, sleeping pills, pain killers, cocaine, heroin, or any variety of mood enhancers or antidepressants that cause them to be numb to the real world. It becomes easier to face each day in their self-made fantasy world than to deal with everyday issues and problems because of their emotional pain. So many people all over the world use these and other means to escape from, or "medicate" their pain.

Alcohol: Individuals who use alcohol to escape into a fantasy-like state often do so to minimize hard situations they are dealing with, i.e. divorce, depression, grief, broken-heartedness, loss of a job, financial problems. Those who use alcohol as an emotional escape and develop habitual drinking problems are often labeled "drunks" or "alcoholics" by some, and by others, are labeled to have a "disease." In all actuality, the condition of these individuals is one of being incapable of coping with the reality of their own lives. Unfortunately, as with drugs—both non-prescription and prescription—the more their bodies take in, the more they need in order to maintain the level of euphoria they initially experienced, thus resulting in drug and alcohol addiction and abuse.

Romance Novels and Soap Operas: Living vicariously through the characters portrayed in romance novels and soap operas is another way of escaping one's reality. If someone is excessively involved in reading romance novels and watching television soap operas, several things can happen. They can begin to look at their own life and relationships through the prism of the characters they are reading about and/or watching; they may begin to live vicariously through the characters, thereby engaging a fantasy or pseudo world; or, they may begin to act out their fantasies, outside of the framework of Biblical and Godly covenant. In each of these, there is the propensity for an increase of bitterness, dissatisfaction, and unrealistic expectations in relationships. Single individuals can develop an unrealistic and warped sense of marriage and relationship that will cause them to seek and find sexual fulfillment prematurely.

Fantasy Role-Playing Games: Excessive amounts of time spent on computer, video, or board games are all indicators—mostly observed in teenagers and young adults—that one is engaged in a form of fantasy living. While these individuals are online, sitting in front of their computer monitor, or raptly engaged with their television screens and handheld game controls, or sitting around a board game, they escape their own lives and become emotionally detached from everything around them. There is the real potential of them taking on the personalities of their characters, and this pseudo-reality, to them, becomes their new reality. They can become social reprobates, unable to interact and participate in real life with real people and real situations. In the real world, they merely *exist*. These types of fantasy role-playing games have been the cause of negative aggression and criminal activity towards those "on the outside" of their fantasy world.[6]

5. Unhealthy and unnatural desires and attractions to people, places, and things

If you find yourself interested, tempted, pulled towards, or attracted to certain things you know, as a Believer, are not pleasing to God and are not in accordance to God's will for your life, you are likely dealing with some form of soul tie. In this instance, you feel the need and drive to seek out whatever that soul tie represents in your life. Don't see it as "just a

---

[6] Some researchers claim that these violent games may cause more intense feelings of aggression than nonviolent games, and may trigger feelings of anger and hostility. Several studies that have supported such findings (see Anderson & Bushman (2001) for a meta-analysis).The theoretical explanations for these types of effects can be explained by a myriad of theories social cognitive theory, excitation transfer theory, priming effect and the general aggression model. Exposure to violent video games has been found to decrease prosocial behaviors including activities such as giving to charity, volunteering and overall "helping" behaviors (Chambers & Ascione, 1987; Wiegman & Schie, 1998). Other researchers have claimed that exposure to violent video games has predicted alcohol consumption, destruction of school property, and other delinquent behaviors (Anderson & Dill, 2000). http://en.wikipedia.org/wiki/Video_game_effects

bad habit." See it for what it is: an indicator of a soul tie operating in your life. This can involve a list of things, too numerous to mention here. We will certainly touch on these more as we move forward.

6. Lack of good judgment and discernment

When you become a Believer, your spirit man takes headship over your life. However, whenever a soul tie is affecting your life in an adverse way, your soul switches places with your spirit man and becomes the authoritative voice in your life.

When I counsel people who are going through a crisis or turmoil in their life, I always instruct them not to make any major decisions while in this emotional state. Crisis and chaos have a way of clouding our thinking and not allowing us to see things as they truly are. One of the things I say is, "I strongly recommend that you do not make any major decisions right now, until, one, the dust around you completely clears, and two, you have found a peaceful place and a season to be in prayer and ask God to show you clearly what you are supposed to do."

Most people who make decisions while in turmoil, confusion, and chaos usually make the wrong decision because they are dealing with emotions, which are a "soulish" thing. If there is a soul tie involved, their soul is not even their own, so they are in no position to discern or to use good judgment, especially as relates to life decisions.

7. Inability to establish and maintain proper relationships

Again, the term "codependent" is important here. Codependency is a state where two people are entirely dependent upon one another at a very unhealthy and soulish level. As adults, it means they can't have a proper, functioning, adult relationship because things are out of order and operating under extreme dysfunction. An example would be this: have you ever known someone (family member, friend, co-worker) that always involves themselves in relationships with the opposite sex and inevitably gets hurt, abused, and disappointed? You know the type. What their soul is longing for is affection, affirmation, companionship, and a sense of "I am worth something." This person will enter into a sinful and disingenuous relationship in search of a missing piece that they, in fact, left bound to another relationship perhaps many years ago. Their soul was split, leaving them in a condition where every relationship they engage in ends up using and hurting them all over again.

8. Incapable of committing to people or things

A soul tie may cause you to be unable to give yourself completely to someone or something. The soul tie causes what is referred to as a "split soul." At some point in time, there was an event or experience that caused you to leave a part of yourself with another person or entity. A trauma, a tragedy, or an emotional separation caused your soul to be partitioned, or "split," leaving you in an incomplete state. Basically, one part of your soul belongs to one person and another part of your soul belongs to someone else or something else somewhere else. This "splitting" of the soul causes a shutting down effect: emotionally, mentally, socially, and even spiritually. Once that part of you is shut down, you no longer possess the ability to commit to people or things. A part of the soul is lost, and out of fear and self-preservation, you may never commit to anything that will "take" from you or "cost" you something.

UNFULFILLED REALITIES

Do you have dreams for your life that you have never seen come to pass? Have you ever received a promise from God? How about this: have you ever received a prophetic word from God that has not yet manifested? There can be times when we receive a true prophetic word by a proven minister, but it never manifests in our life. Does it mean the giver of the prophetic word just missed it? It is possible. But it could also be that even though that word was right on, there is something in our life that has us hooked or tied down, or something in our past that is disallowing us to find our way to that word. Prophecy deals with the future. When a prophetic word is given, that word is in our future waiting on us to get there. It may be in

93

our near future or it may be for years to come, but it is there. The problem could be that we are so deeply anchored to the ties of our past we are rendered ineffective in our pursuit of achieving and walking in what God has said about our present and our future.

The Bible says that God's Word **cannot** return to Him void, without accomplishing what it was sent to accomplish (Isaiah 55:11). God's Word concerning your life is true. It is eternal. He will see to it that it is performed. Our job is to identify and remove every limiting factor and hindering force that is keeping us from achieving that objective.

TAKING THE NEXT STEP

We are about to move into the specifics of the THREE main categories of soul ties. This is the part where you will begin to identify SPECIFICALLY where these limitations have been established in your life, and where you need to be free.

As you move into the following three chapters, it is important that you do so prayerfully and with an open heart. Everything we have covered until now has been preparing you with knowledge for this moment.

Let me reiterate. A soul tie may not only be with an individual, but can also be with some thing or entity. It can be with a church or an organization. It can be with a thought process or system. Through contracts or other business dealings, it is also possible to form soul ties with companies or institutions.

When you are dealing with an ungodly and unhealthy soul tie, there is a part of your emotions that is incapable of functioning in a healthy and normal manner. The six indicators mentioned previously in this chapter serve as evidence that the soul is in control, and your life is functioning in a way that is incapable of experiencing real progress, true peace, joy, and success.

You are ready now to tackle the tough issues. You have the knowledge, and now we pray that God would, in these next few chapters, illuminate your understanding and awareness of any and all areas where soul ties are restricting the flow and grace of God in your life.

Let's get to work!

CHAPTER 7

Relational
Soul Ties

Most of us, if not all of us, at some point in our lives find ourselves limited by things that tie us to people, things, and situations in our past that are unhealthy and ungodly. The Bible calls them "yokes" or "bonds of wickedness." These **relational soul ties** can be with relationships at any level—family, friends, past romantic relationships, affiliations, previous churches, businesses, or associations. Relational soul ties are one of the most powerful soul ties because they most often deal with those whom we have trusted, loved, and cared for.

DAVID AND JONATHAN

Let's start with some aspects of positive relationships. Not all soul ties are bad. In fact, the story of David and Jonathan depicts a phenomenal picture of a relational soul tie—a good one.

"Now it came about when he had finished speaking to Saul, that the soul of Jonathan was knit to the soul of David, and Jonathan loved him as himself."

1 Samuel 18:1

The Bible says here in 1 Samuel 18 that David was "knit" to the soul of Jonathan. The New International Version of the Bible says, "Jonathan became one in spirit with David." The word "knit" is also translated in the Hebrew as *bound, joined together,* and *tied.*

> Relational soul ties are one of the most powerful soul ties because they most often deal with those whom we have trusted, loved, and cared for.

Their relationship had developed over a period of time and had come to the point where in one moment of time, something very spiritual happened. There was literally a melding together that took place between each of their souls and they literally became as one. As you will read in a moment, their friendship had the characteristics of a wonderful and Godly relationship.

CHARACTERISTICS OF A HEALTHY & GODLY RELATIONSHIP

Sometimes relational soul ties are hard to actually acknowledge because they involve people that are generally close to us in proximity and are around us often. Most often the hardest things to see are those things that are right under our nose.

Examine the relationships you are currently involved with and any previous relationships you have had in the past. As you examine these, I ask that you would weigh each of them against the following five characteristics. In doing this, you will be able to measure whether or not your present and past relationships are healthy, beneficial, and Godly; or, whether they are unhealthy, detrimental, and ungodly. If they are not able to meet these criteria, it is possible that you have identified a relationship, or perhaps relationships, that are negatively impacting your forward movement in life. A soul tie could be developing or may have already been developed in you that is limiting your ability to receive and engage life as God has intended for you.

As you read these please apply them to each relationship you have presently, have had in the past, or are developing right now. Make a note concerning each relationship. We will revisit your list at a later time.

The Five Characteristics of Godly Relationships

1. The people you are relationally involved with are totally committed to your spiritual growth and health. They are just as committed to your spiritual health as they are their own. The opposite is also true. If they are not com-

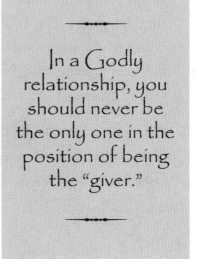

In a Godly relationship, you should never be the only one in the position of being the "giver."

mitted to your spiritual health, it is not a healthy relationship.

2. The people you are relationally involved with are concerned about your overall well-being as much as they are their own or the well-being of their own family.

3. In a Godly relationship, you should never be the only one in the position of being the "giver." Every healthy relationship is two-sided by way of giving and receiving. It must always be reciprocal in nature.

   Have you ever been in a relationship where over the years you have found yourself constantly giving and giving and giving; never finding yourself on the receiving end? Eventually, you will become bankrupt emotionally, spiritually, socially, and many times, economically. You're always giving. Some might say, "Well, it's more blessed to give than to receive." Yes, that's true, but it doesn't say you shouldn't receive. In fact, healthy relationships always reciprocate what they are given. The Bible says, *"Give, and it will be given to you: good measure, pressed down, shaken together, and running over,"* (Luke 6:38, NKJV). The relationship that is Godly gives *and* receives with joy.

4. A Godly relationship does not cause you to violate your conscience or walk against the plan and will of God for your life.

5. A Godly relationship does not manipulate through anger or other emotional abuse; but rather, it motivates through love.

Well, how are you doing? Have you identified any relationships that may fall into the category of unhealthy or ungodly? Be sure to write down the names that came to your mind and any thoughts concerning the relationship(s).

WHEN OUR PAST BECOMES OUR PRESENT

Because of the strong power of covenant, there are many instances where out of past relationships soul ties were formed and have continued beyond the intended life span of the relationship itself. The tie could even be with someone who has since deceased died or someone who has gone on with their life, but your soul is still tied to the memories, the words, the experiences, and the thoughts of what happened between you and that person. As a result, you cannot be free to live your life as God wants you to. **You are literally living in the present from the viewpoint and limitations of the past**. While "in time" we have moved on, our lives are still being affected by the soulish things of the past relationship.

THE LAW OF ASSOCIATION

Proverbs 13:20 says this:

> *"He that walks with wise men will be wise, but the companion of fools will suffer harm, (or destruction)."*

Your life will rise or fall to the level of your associations and relationships. When I associate myself with individuals who are not headed in the same direction I desire to go, I

101

limit my ability to get there! Do you understand this principle? When I engage in meaningful relationships, they either build or enhance my life, or they will drag me down to their level of thinking and functioning. If you want to know where you are going in life, just look at your friends!

Here is the most frightening part of this equation: years after I have severed my day-to-day association with a person, if I have not dealt with the soul tie that was developed during the lifetime of that relationship, I continue to be affected by everything that is taking place in that individual's world! I may be thousands of miles away and have not spoken to them in years, but we continue to "relate" by virtue of the soul tie that is in place.

> *"Do not be deceived and misled! Evil (ungodly) companionships (communion, associations) corrupt and deprave good manners and moral character."*

> **1 Corinthians 15:33 (AMP)**

Let me define the term "ungodly" in the context of this teaching. Anything that is ungodly can be viewed as *disconnected from God; antagonistic to God and his will; detrimental to the plans and purposes of God in one's life; and absent of the qualities and characteristics of God.*

With that understanding, please see this: when I engage with ungodly relationships; when I associate with individuals who are not concerned about God's plans for my life; and when I associate myself with people, places, or institutions that are working contrary to what God has said about me, it will affect my character, my morals, and ultimately, my ability to perform at my God given potential.

CHECK THE FRUIT

"You will know them by their fruits. Grapes are not gathered from thorn bushes nor figs from thistles, are they? So every good tree bears good fruit, but the bad tree bears bad fruit. A good tree cannot produce bad fruit, nor can a bad tree produce good fruit."

Matthew 7:16-18

This scripture is so important. It portrays a very simple yet profound principle. When we see certain fruit (or results) continually and consistently manifesting in our lives, we must decide, after measuring it against God's Word to us, if it is good fruit or bad fruit. If the results we continue to see produced in our lives are bad, then according to this principle, we can safely and rightly judge that a *bad tree* is producing this fruit. The problem is that we continue to nurture and cater to the bad tree, hoping that through some strange twist of fate, the fruit will morph into something productive and good. No! A thousand times no! When there is a bad tree in the orchard of our life, it must be cut down,

> When there is a bad tree in the orchard of our life, it must be cut down, removed, and completely eliminated.

removed, and completely eliminated. We must go after the *roots*, and make sure that this tree will no longer affect the quality of the crop we are producing. This is why we must deal with relational soul ties. Bad fruit—bad tree!

WHO ARE YOU YOKED WITH?

"Do not be bound (or yoked) together with unbelievers; for what partnership have righteousness and lawlessness, or what fellowship has light and darkness?

2 Corinthians 6:14

I want to look at this scripture very closely, because within its context is one of the most powerful things I have ever seen regarding relational soul ties. Let's look at the deeper meaning of several of the key words here.

"BOUND OR YOKED TOGETHER"

The Greek word for this is "heterozyge," which is translated *to come under an unequal or different yoke, or to be unequally yoked.* Also, it means to fellowship with one who is not equal to or in agreement with.

What this is saying here is simple:

♦ Do not come under any yoke or authority that is unequal to the anointing, calling, and destiny of your life.

♦ Do not bind yourself to something or someone that will limit you due to the unequal nature of their life, belief, and destiny.

♦ Do not fellowship or bind yourself to someone who is not equal to or in agreement with what God has said concerning your life and future.

♦ Do not unite with someone who is not going where God desires to take you. They will cripple your ability to move with Him.

♦ A *yoke* is a wooden instrument that BINDS two oxen together. Its purpose is to cause them to only be able to walk TOGETHER. Imagine trying to move on with your life in a new and Godly direction, while being YOKED together with someone or something that is moving in an opposite direction. It creates strife, confusion, guilt, frustration, anger, and countless other negative emotions and experiences.

♦ If you yoke with someone or something that is not committed to what God has said about your life, when they move in a contrary direction, you have no choice but to move with them. You want to go left, but they take you right!

♦ If they make bad decisions and find themselves in serious circumstance, you too feel the pain and struggle of where they have taken you.

♦ Why? Because you are unequally yoked!

"PARTNERSHIP"

In Greek this is *metoche*. It is translated: *sharing, communion or fellowship*. What kind of communion can there actually be

105

between good and evil; God's plan for my life and the plans of others?

"RIGHTEOUSNESS"

The Greek word used here is *dikaiosynē*. It is translated in a broad sense as the state of him who is as he ought to be, in a condition acceptable to God. It is the doctrine concerning the way in which man may attain a state that is approved of God. It is also known as *integrity; virtue; purity of life; rightness; correctness of thinking; and feeling and acting in alignment with God's plan and ordinance.* All of this being said, righteousness is that state of being where we are *thinking* like God and in accordance to His will and plan for our lives.

"LAWLESSNESS"

Anomia is the Greek term for "lawlessness." "Anomia" is translated as *unrighteousness (or incorrect thinking), ignorant of the law of God, and refusal to submit to the law and plans of God.*

"FELLOWSHIP"

The Greek word is *koinonia* and it is translated as *fellowship, association, community, communion, joint participation, the right hand as a sign of fellowship.*

"LIGHT"

The Greek word for "light" is *phos*. It is translated *to shine or make manifest, of truth and its knowledge, together with the spiritual purity associated with it; that which is exposed to the view of all, openly, publicly*. If you have light, you have the ability to reason, your mind is able to see and comprehend, and you possess the power to understand truth as God sees it!

"DARKNESS"

The word for "darkness" is translated from the Greek *skotos*. It means *darkened eyesight or blindness; ignorance (or inability) to discern divine things and the accompanying ungodliness that comes from such darkness; persons in whom such darkness becomes obvious and has impact.*

Understanding the deeper meanings of these words brings us to this point. If I am to benefit from the Light of God; if I am to see my way clearly into the fullness and complete scope of destiny that God has created for me; if I am to experience the blessing, the favor, and the anointings that God has spoken over my life, it is imperative that I disassociate myself from all darkness, all influences, and all relationships that are contrary to God's plans for my life. Not only do I stop hanging out with or spending time with darkness, but I break the emotional and spiritual ties that have formed between me and those people or things that represent darkness in my life. It is only when I break these ties that bind that I am allowed to come out of the darkness and move into His marvelous light (1 Peter 2:9).

> *". . . Any city or house divided against itself will not stand."*
>
> **Matthew 12:25**

"The eye is the lamp of the body; so then if your eye is clear, your whole body will be full of light. But if your eye is bad, your whole body will be full of darkness. If then the light that is in you is darkness, how great is that darkness."

Matthew 6:22-23

It is impossible to find success and fulfillment if we are attempting to operate with one foot in light and the other in darkness. We cannot expect the Word of God, the blessing of God, and the favor of God to operate in our lives as long as we are tied to people, systems, ideas, and thoughts that are dark in their nature. God, in all of His greatness, will not be found in a place where darkness is welcome.

PERSONAL ASSESSMENT - A CLOSER LOOK

We must begin to examine our hearts, our minds, and our lives to see if there are any relational soul ties that are affecting our life today. Here is a list that may help you to remember or identify something or someone *in your present or your past* that is limiting you in this season.

- ◆ Old relationships/friendships
- ◆ Gifts received that carried emotional collateral
- ◆ Experiences with friend(s)
- ◆ Old jobs
- ◆ Old churches

- Old anointings

- Ungodly or sin-filled relationships

- People who don't want to see you succeed, but you are still tied to them

- People who do not love you

- People who are not walking after God

- People who are financially insolvent or struggling

TAKE TIME NOW

- Ask God to reveal to you any and all relationships (past and present) that may in some way be adversely affecting you today.

- Ask the Holy Spirit to show you what areas of your life are being impacted by these soul ties.

- Ask God to CLEARLY teach and instruct you how to be free as we go through this process.

Father, I pray now for my brother and my sister, that You would cause their hearts and their spirits to open to new revelation and new insight. May they feel the arms of a loving Father embracing them and comforting them as they walk through the sometimes painful process of uprooting these matters. Reveal now, Oh Lord, any and all relational soul ties that are inhibiting the growth and progress of Your child. Open our eyes that we may see what You see. Help us to be free, in Jesus' name. Amen.

CHAPTER 8

Sexual Soul Ties

As we probe into this chapter dealing with sexual soul ties, let me first say that sexual soul ties have been and still are today wreaking havoc and destruction on lives, marriages, and families. Many of the emotional and psychological problems that plague our society can be traced directly to some sort of sexual misconduct that has created an ungodly soul tie. There are countless victims of child sexual abuse, rape, incest; as well as individuals that have participated in premarital and extramarital sexual relationships, and other things that we will not necessarily cover in this book. Those who have been the victim or the willing participant in these types of sexual misconduct are living out their lives not only under the weight of the tremendous emotional burden, but also within the confines of a sexual soul tie. These wounded, fragmented, soul-bound individuals stumble into marriages and families and continue to stagger through life, often leaving destruction in their wake.

TWENTY-FIRST CENTURY SEXUAL REVOLUTION

The day in which we now live is very different from when I was a teenager and young adult. There has been an extreme shift in the social norms of our society, especially in terms of things that deal with sexual behavior. It's both disturbing and frightening to me to see that moral our culture is facing a drastic downward spiral. Things that were once considered "taboo" are now just as normal as eating an ice cream cone. What is aired on television that once would have offended even a pagan, non-Christian person is now considered acceptable for our teens and preteens to watch. Casual sex outside of the bonds of marriage is just as accepted as dating and holding hands once was. The times have changed and the consequences are enormous.

The consequences of this extreme shift in sexual mores and norms of our society are far-reaching and include everything from increased prevalence of sexually transmitted diseases to the literally hundreds of thousands of rape and sexual assault incidents to the more than forty-six million abortions that are performed worldwide every year. There really is no way to measure the tremendous negative impact our deteriorating sexual morality has had on the world and on the millions of lives that have been affected by them in one way or another. While agencies throughout the world attempt to quantify this social catastrophe by compiling statistics, the damage in human terms is incalculable. The numbers provided to us by these agencies give us a mere glimpse of the magnitude of this moral epidemic.

In the United States of America, where I live, the statistics are staggering. The Center for Disease Control estimates that approximately 19 million new infections of sexually transmitted diseases occur each year. Almost half of the cases of STDs reported occur among young people between fifteen and twenty-four years old. That's almost 10 million teenagers and young adults that are infected with an STD annually! While the physical and psychological effects of STDs are profound, these diseases also exact a tremendous economic toll. Direct medical costs associated with STDs in the United States are estimated at up to $14.7 billion annually.[7]

The United States has the highest incidence of reported rapes for countries that report such data. Information from the National Women's Study, a longitudinal telephone survey of a sample of women at least eighteen years of age, show approximately 683,000 women are forcibly raped each year.[8] Of that number eighty-three percent are under the age of twenty-four.[9] And these numbers represent only the reported rapes and sexual assaults. There is no way to determine how many rapes and other acts of sexual violence go unreported each year.

It's estimated that 46 million abortions are performed throughout the world every year. In America alone, there are approximately 1.37 million legal abortions performed annually. What makes this number even more disturbing is that twenty percent, or approximately 275,000, of those abortions are per-

[7] http://www.cdc.gov/std/stats/trends2006.htm

[8] http://www.paralumun.com/issuesrapestats.htm

[9] http://www.oak.cats.ohiou.edu/~ad361896/anne/cease.html

formed on teenage girls; more than 16,000 on girls under the age of fifteen.[10] Ninety-three percent of all abortions in the United States—1.27 million—are performed for "social reasons," meaning the child is "inconvenient" or "unwanted."[11] To say that these numbers are staggering is a gross understatement. The widespread, long-term effects of increased sexual activity and moral decline are immeasurable.

Not only has sexual activity become accepted, it has become an expected behavior among teenagers the world over. The pressure to become sexually active is great. Just a few short years ago, when a teenager engaged in sexual activity, they were looked down on and, to some degree, scorned or ostracized. Nowadays, there has been a drastic, moral shift that has completely reversed that stand. In today's culture, if a teenager is a virgin, they are the exception, and can find themselves on the receiving end of the teasing, isolation, and unfair pressure, which many times drives our children to make decisions they regret for the rest of their lives. This state of affairs is a tragedy and a cultural catastrophe. It is messed up! The sad truth of the matter is that we—as parents, the Church, and society—have allowed ourselves to be lulled to sleep, and at the same time, we have opened the door for Satan to entangle our children with soul ties that endanger their lives, their destinies, and their future.

THE MEDIA MONSTER

Hollywood, as a whole, has lured and captured a generation of our young people through various forms of media including music, television, the big screen, and now—the added threat

---

[10] http://www.abortionno.org/Resources/fastfacts.html
[11] Ibid.

to innocence—the Internet. While the Internet can be one of the most influential and effective tools used in ministry today, it has also become a powerful tool being used to steal the innocence and minds of our children, exposing them (and us), to even deeper levels of debauchery and sin. The Internet affects every age group, ethnicity, gender, and socioeconomic class of people. My ministry requires that I travel extensively throughout the world every year. Having stayed in more hotel rooms than I can begin to count, there is one prominent piece of furniture that dominates the entire room—the television. I had to make a decision a long time ago that when I stayed in a hotel room, I would guard my heart and my eyes—not just from the pay channels, but the regular cable channels as well. If you have cable or satellite television in your home, you must be ever diligent concerning the materials and content you allow into your home. Your home is a sanctuary for your family. Even while channel surfing, a brief glimpse can cause images to be forever implanted in the subconscious; unintentionally causing lasting soul ties that wreak havoc in the mind for years to come.

I could go on to name show after show, sitcom after sitcom, and in recent years, many movies that are laced with an agenda to desensitize us to sexual sin. Just understand this: if you willingly allow the spirits that are transferred from these inappropriate programs to enter your area of dominion area (your home), those spirits and the ties that go with them will cause you to crave more and more. Do not entertain spirits that come through the television! Guard your heart. Guard your mind. Guard your children. Monitor what they are watching. Is a moment of entertainment worth the destiny of one child? Never!

THE POWER OF THE PRINTED PAGE

Carol Burnett, a famous U.S. television actress/comedienne once said, *"Words, once they are printed, have a life of their own."* She couldn't have been more accurate. Reading—whether you're reading the Bible, romance novels, Christian inspirational books, fiction or non-fiction horror, horoscopes, New Age or occult books, magazines—can and will create soulish ties. These materials open your soul, gaining emotional access to you, and thereby affect the way you think, decide, and respond to life in every area. In addition, by opening your heart and mind to these things, soul ties that already exist are strengthened and reinforced. They literally take on a life of their own once you have allowed them to assimilate into the deep parts of your mind. I ministered to a lady once who, in her early preteen years, became addicted to reading those small, paperback romance novels. She couldn't get enough of them. It wasn't long before she began to live vicariously through the characters in the novels and began to fantasize about the situations in each book. Never having experienced anything romantically or sexually herself, she began to be lured by curiosity into a dark world of fantasy love relationships. The idea of having an affair and satisfying herself with "forbidden fruit" became very enticing to her; to the point that she began formulating plans on how she could experience it for herself. As a result, she became very disillusioned and deceived.

The words on the pages of those books not only took on a life of their own, but they actually *took over* her life and consumed her. They planted seeds in her heart, images in her mind, and ties to a dark world. They haunted her for years, until she realized what they were and the power they had over her life. She began to understand where and how they were rooted. As she began to learn the principles in this book, she came to a clear awareness, and today is free from their ungodly and destructive effects.

Remember, the mind and the thoughts are an integral part of the soul. When things such as these capture your mind, they have your soul as well. A couple of years ago, I took my son into a large, well-known bookstore/café to buy a particular reader for a class he had at school. As we were checking out at the counter, right there in front of us—in front of him—were all kinds of illicit magazines. There were trendy, popular magazines along with ones that were lesser known, but just as crude and inappropriate. Eye level to where he was standing, was the front cover of a magazine, with a photograph of a bare-naked woman. The only things covered on her body were her genital area and the most private parts of her breasts. We have always taught our children to guard their hearts, but what is a young boy to do? My ten-year-old son standing at my side did what any boy would do at that moment. I pulled him aside and say to him, "Son, listen to me. You are a child of God, and you are destined for greatness. We will not allow Satan to attach this image to your heart. Protect your heart. Protect your eyes. We cannot look at this and allow it inside." It wasn't his fault. He did not choose to be exposed. However, Satan will use every opportunity to get a hook in your soul. We must be aware!

From that day on, I decided I would not darken the doors of that bookstore or those like them. I refuse to support a company or business that is propagating the agenda of Satan himself; an agenda of dumbing down and desensitizing our society and culture and making sex a casual and acceptable experience for anyone, any age, anywhere, anytime. You might say, "Well, that's a bit overboard, don't you think?" No, I don't! Actually, I don't think it's strong enough. Sexual promiscuity is a cancer in our world, and it is systematically destroying the lives of men, women, boys, and girls. We must take a stand. We must guard our hearts. We must take back the destinies that have been stolen or interfered with by this deadly onslaught.

PROMISCUITY – ITS RELENTLESS DEBT

Many Christians have been saved out of a promiscuous life-style—you may be one of them. Romans 8:1 says, *"There is therefore now no condemnation for those who are in Christ Jesus."* There is no condemnation or criticism here; only a testimony to the grace of God on your life. However, long after you have been redeemed from that lifestyle, the soul ties that remain as a result of that lifestyle will still pull on you. Unless dealt with, they can, *and will*, continue to require draws upon your life— many of which you cannot afford.

It is so important that we guard our hearts, our eyes, our ears, and our minds as it relates to what we read, watch on television, and to everything that we put into our spirit via our physical senses. If you have ever lived a lifestyle where you have been with multiple partners— whether it be two, ten, or a hundred—it makes no difference. You carry with you a part of that person's soul, and in turn, you have given a part of your soul to them. Depending on where they are, who they are, what they're doing, and what they're experiencing in their life, you are being affected every single day in your own relationships and in every facet of your life—past, present, and future. The fact is that person now possesses a part of your soul.

"Do you not know that your bodies are members of Christ? Shall I then take away the members of Christ and make them members of a prostitute? May it never be! {16} Or do you not know that the one who joins himself to a prostitute is one body with her? For He says, 'THE TWO SHALL BECOME ONE FLESH.' {17} But the one who joins himself to the Lord is one spirit with Him."

1 Corinthians 6:15-17

THE MARRIAGE COVENANT

Anytime we begin to talk on the subject of the marriage covenant, it is important that we go to the beginning. When a concept or principle is mentioned or alluded to for the first time in Scripture, it establishes a precedent or framework which will apply when that same principle or concept is mentioned again. This is what we refer to as the Law of First Mention.

We should apply this "law" to the concept of marriage to see how God intended it to be.

> *"God created man in His own image, in the image of God He created him; male and female He created them."*

Genesis 1:27

We see by this scripture that God created Man—there meaning "Mankind"—both male and female. Then in the following chapter, He separated them making them male and female, individually.

> *"So the Lord God caused a deep sleep to fall upon the man, and he slept; then He took one of his ribs and closed up the flesh at that place. {22} The Lord God fashioned into a woman the rib which He had taken from the man, and brought her to the man. {23} The man said, 'This is now bone of my bones, and flesh of my flesh; she shall be called Woman, because she was taken out of Man.'"*

Genesis 2:21-23

Up until that time, they were one. When man was separated from God in the Garden, it created a fracture in the relationship between God and Man. Since Man (male and female) was created in His image, this fracture would be reflected in the earth as well. The entire dynamic of that relationship changed. No longer were male and female one just because they were created of God. Now, they were two individuals who had to form a union through covenant in order that they might be positioned together as one.

The Word of God only honors sexual activity between a man and a woman within the confines and the covenant of marriage. Anything outside of that, God and His Word reject, and cannot sanction or bless. Look what Paul said to the Hebrews about marriage:

"Marriage is to be held in honor among all, and the marriage bed is to be undefiled; for fornicators and adulterers God will judge."

Hebrews 13:4

That word "undefiled" there means that the bed of the marriage covenant cannot be dishonored. The honor of the institution of marriage between one man and one woman should not be defiled. Other words for "defiled" are *tainted, corrupted, degraded*; therefore, something that is "undefiled" is *pure, clean,* and *uncontaminated.* The bed of the marriage covenant is pure in God's sight. The relationship between a man and a woman is to be one of leaving and "cleaving." As the King James Version of the Bible says it: *"Therefore a man shall leave his father and mother and shall cleave unto his wife,"* (Genesis 2:24). The word "cleave" has the connotation of adhering to (as by an adhesive), clinging to, and following closely. A more modern translation of this same passage of scripture helps us understand the idea of cleaving to one's spouse.

"For this reason a man shall leave his father and his mother, and be joined to his wife; and they shall become one flesh."

Genesis 2:24

Other definitions for "cleave" are, *to overtake, pursue hard, stick together, and take.* In considering this concept of cleaving (or being bound to), let's look at a passage in Genesis which gives us a picture of how this works.

"Now Dinah the daughter of Leah, whom she had borne to Jacob, went out to visit the daughters of the land. {2} When Shechem the son of Hamor the Hivite, the prince of the land, saw her, he took her and lay with her by force. {3} He was deeply attracted to Dinah the daughter of Jacob, and he loved the girl and spoke tenderly to her. {4} So Shechem spoke to his father Hamor, saying, "Get me this young girl for a wife." {5} Now Jacob heard that he had defiled Dinah his daughter; but his sons were with his livestock in the field, so Jacob kept silent until they came in."

Genesis 34:1-5

"But Hamor spoke with them, saying, 'The soul of my son Shechem longs for your daughter; please give her to him in marriage.'"

Genesis 34:8

Simply put, Shechem raped and defiled Dinah, which, even given the horrible circumstances, created a soul tie between them that was insatiable and overwhelming. His appetite had been awakened by sexual relations with her, even though it was not consensual, and now he was consumed with having her as his own. He craved for more, so much to the point that his father felt it necessary to intervene and ask for her to be his wife on his behalf.

This example brings forth a powerful point that I feel I must make. Statistics show us that a significant percentage of people have been sexually abused, raped, or taken advantage of in some form. Most recent studies by the Rape, Abuse & Incest National Network suggest that every two and a half minutes, someone in the United States of America, where I live, is sexually assaulted. These same studies reveal that one in every six women and one in every thirty-three men are victims of sexual assault.[12] In America, more than eighty thousand cases of child sexual abuse are reported every year, but experts believe this number is not truly representative of the actual occurrence. The number of unreported instances of child sexual abuse is probably much greater because children are usually afraid to tell anyone what has happened. The long-term emotional and psychological damage to the child—and then the adult—can be overwhelming.[13] As horrific and as painfully devastating as this is, it is important to understand that these encounters also form soul ties, even if the act we experienced is against our will.

I will never forget the Sunday morning service at Covenant International Worship Center when, as we were taking

[12] http://www.rainn.org/statistics/index.html
[13] http://www.aacap.org/cs/root/facts_for_families/child_sexual_abuse

our church congregation through this teaching on sexual soul ties, the Holy Spirit prompted me to have a special altar call for any individual who may have been raped or who experienced some form of sexual abuse at some point in their life. I knew the Lord was leading me, however, I could have never anticipated what happened next.

In my mind, I anticipated one or two might respond, but to my amazement, somewhere between fifteen and twenty of these precious people, both men and women, began running to the front, weeping; some were screaming out, as God delivered and healed them one by one. It was a miraculous moment as we watched God reverse years of pain, shame, guilt, and brokenness, and break forever the ties that had bound these beloved children of God.

ADULTERY, PREMARITAL SEX, AND SOUL TIES

If you have ever had any type of relationship or intimacy with someone other than your spouse that was of a sexual nature, you must know and recognize that with each relationship, a very powerful and deep soul tie was formed. Those ties literally possess the power and force to prohibit you, or at the very least, limit you, in your quest to reach and live out the destiny God has planned for you.

Let's take it one step further. If you are or have been *emotionally* involved in an intimate relationship with someone outside your marriage—even if nothing physical or sexual has taken place—it is possible, and in my opinion, likely, that soul ties have formed with those individuals that are keeping you from completely giving yourself emotionally to your spouse.

Go back a little further in your life. It may be that you experienced a sexual encounter as a teenager, or possibly multiple encounters. What about those crazy, care-free college days? Consider the activities and relationships you participated in during that time of your life. In any case, if you ever engaged in premarital sex, soul ties were formed, and they are at work in your life today.

For some, soul ties may have been formed because of an extra-marital (adulterous) relationship, a homosexual relationship from your past, a relationship from earlier in your adult life, or even a relationship you may be having now. In any sexual relationship—past or present—experienced outside the auspices of covenantal marriage between a woman and a man, soul ties are formed between **your** soul and the soul of the person with whom you have had, or are having, the relationship. Because of this, you will be plagued with a craving and a desire to seek out and find what your soul has cleaved to, or has been tied to. You will continually be drawn into a web and pattern of

> Soul ties transcend the salvation experience and pass through the cross unchanged, until we address them and deal with them out of our free will.

destructive behavior, never realizing your full potential, nor God's vision for your life.

Whether or not you were saved at the time the relationship took place is irrelevant. Soul ties transcend the salvation experience and pass through the cross unchanged, until **we** address them and deal with them out of our free will. Remember, when we become born again, our spirit man is made new but we still have to contend with our soul (our mind, will, and emotions), and of course, our flesh. We have to engage in the process of continually renewing our mind according to the Word.

> *"If indeed you have heard Him and have been taught in Him, just as truth is in Jesus, {22} that, in reference to your former manner of life, you lay aside the old self, which is being corrupted in accordance with the lusts of deceit, {23} and that you be renewed in the spirit of your mind, {24} and put on the new self, which in the likeness of God has been created in righteousness and holiness of the truth."*

Ephesians 4:21-24

You say, "I would never think about being unfaithful to my spouse," or "I would never have sex before I get married." I'm telling you right now, if you are a man or a woman and you've ever had sexual relations with somebody outside of the marriage covenant, until it is addressed and healed, there is something in your soul that is reaching out everywhere you go. If the soul tie with that individual—or individuals—is not dealt with, you will live with the struggles and the consequences of the soul tie day after day, year after year. Those ties must be severed and broken off of you if you are to truly live and be free.

You see, sin ties us to things, people, places, events, and situations. There are cords of sin that have wrapped themselves like tentacles around our soul and our spirit and yet we wonder why we go through seasons where we feel like we're being pulled back into harmful, "old-man" things. Our spirit is saying, "No," and yet our flesh is saying, "Yes." There is a tug-of-war being played out between our renewed spirit and our carnal flesh with our soul being right in the middle of the fight.

In the church community we have called it by various names and labels, such as, "temptation," "spirits pulling on us," or "having bad or impure thoughts." Here is what it is: it is actually our soul longing, craving, and desiring for that thing you tasted before which has never been cut off. It is the soul pulling you toward the source of the tie and its devices.

> Each time you have sexual relations with someone, or involve yourself in an emotional affair outside of marriage, a piece of the paper—a piece of your soul—is torn off and given to that individual.

SCATTERED PIECES

Imagine, if you will, that I am holding a single piece of paper before you. This piece of paper represents one hundred percent of your soul and your heart: your love, your life, your everything. As you go through life, you make choices—choices that cause your soul to be fragmented, distributed, and even broken. Each time you have sexual relations with someone, or involve yourself in an emotional affair outside of marriage, a piece of the paper—*a piece of your soul*—is torn off and given to that individual. The depth and scope of each relationship in great part determines the portion of your soul that is left with that person.

One by one, fragments of your soul are torn off and given to people. Then, the day comes when you are to be united with the person God has chosen for you, and without realizing it, all you have left to give is a very small and broken part of your heart and soul. At the place of covenant, the altar of marriage, you are incapable of giving your all, because "your all" no longer belongs to you. There are parts of your soul scattered all over the country; living in homes that you don't own; working at offices you have no connection to; in other relationships you are not directly connected to. There are pieces of you out there everywhere.

If **each** of these pieces of paper that are torn off represents one individual out there, ask yourself this question: what are those people going through? Well, this person struggles constantly with depression—and we wonder, "Why do I struggle seasonally with being depressed?" Another person over here is cursed with poverty and can never make any money. They are always broke and even if they make money, their pockets have holes in them. You name it, claim it, blab it and grab it, yet ask,

"Why can't I break through into some financial prosperity?" Another person is dealing with the effects of a generational curse—cancer. All of a sudden, you hit thirty-five, forty, fifty years of age and without explanation, cancer shows up in your body and defiantly rears its ugly head at you—when in your family, there is no cancer. Hmm . . . Does it sound ridiculous?

Soul ties have attached themselves to our lives and have tied us to other people and their problems. We must break free and recapture the pieces of our soul. I am a living witness to the fact that God can put the pieces back together!

For those of us who are married, is it any wonder why marriages are struggling and going through vicious cycles of discontent and despair? Is it any surprise that more than fifty percent of Americans who get married end up in divorce court? You see, marriage involves something that is called a covenant. A covenant is a binding contract which involves blood. It's not just a simple promise to do something. A covenant is much deeper than that. It literally connects heart to heart, soul to soul, and body to body. In the covenant of marriage, when you stand at the altar and exchange your vows, there are three voices that agree to your covenant: you, your spouse, and God Himself.

BONE OF MY BONE

"The man said, 'This is now <u>bone</u> of my bones, and <u>flesh</u> of my flesh: she shall be called Woman, because she was taken out of man.' For this reason a man shall

leave his father and mother, and be joined to his wife; and they shall become one flesh."

Genesis 2:23-24

In this passage, Adam uses interesting terminology to describe the relationship with his wife. He says, "She is bone of my bones, and flesh of my flesh." What does this mean, and how does this help us understand this **oneness** concept?

"Bone" is the Hebrew word *"etsem,"* which means *self-same essence or substance, or life; the essence or essential nature of a thing, a marker of which something consists as the same.*

The word translated here as "flesh" is the Hebrew word *"basar,"* which is interpreted, *body, complete entire body, including the total person.* It is also interpreted *kin,* or *myself.*

In other words, Adam was saying, "You are now the selfsame essence or substance as I am; we are one and the same; we are one body; one life; we are marked as one. When I look at you, I see myself!"

MARRIAGES ENDING IN DIVORCE

The marriage covenant involves oneness; the kind of oneness Adam exclaimed when he first laid eyes on the woman God had created. You cannot be one with your spouse if there are still pieces of your soul scattered about. If you have ever been married in the past, or if since you have been married you have given part of your soul to somebody and you have not yet redeemed those pieces, you are incapable of giving your whole being to anyone.

You say, "Right before I got married I got saved and was filled with the Spirit of God, and I repented of all that. I dealt with my sin and I know that I am forgiven." I understand that, and that is one hundred percent correct. However, what you must know and understand is that there is another step you need to take. You need to take the step now of repossessing the parts of you that were given to somebody else outside of Godly covenant, and bringing those back into yourself so that you can give it to the person you have now made covenant with. You may be saying with your mouth, "I give you all of me," but you don't have all of you to give!

HOMOSEXUALITY & SOUL TIES

I feel it is important to address the struggle of homosexuality. It seems that we are embattled on every side to embrace the idea that same sex relationships and same sex marriages are acceptable and right. While the purpose of this book is not to address this specific matter, the context of this chapter demands that I do so.

God created the marriage institution as a means to fill the earth with a people who would rule and manage the earth as His legal representatives. He created male and female, husband and wife, man and woman. Marriage is constituted by God as a union between one man, and one woman. Period. Any "union" or sexual relationship outside of the Biblical mandate for marriage is unacceptable to God and cannot be sanctioned or blessed.

With that said, I want to make it clear that healing and wholeness is available to every individual who is willing to allow God into his or her heart to work. He will lead you on a journey of freedom. For those that have once embraced the homosexual lifestyle and have found freedom (and there are many), it is important for you to know that soul ties work exactly the same for all of us. The principles we have covered in this chapter are true for you today! You, too, can be free of the ties that bind you and continue to cause you pain and limitations.

CLOSING THOUGHTS

I know that at this moment many of you are experiencing the voice of God speaking to you. You recognize that there are soul ties in this area that you must address. Here is what I encourage you to do:

- ♦ Write down the names of every individual you can remember with whom you may have formed a sexual soul tie.

- ♦ Note the feelings and the emotions that remembering this person causes you.

- ♦ If you are able, note the areas in your life that you feel are being directly affected by these sexual soul ties.

You are almost there. I know it's painful right now, but let's keep walking this out. God is with you. He is helping you. You will be free and you will know joy like never before.

Father, I am asking that at this very moment You hold this precious person. Let them feel the security and confidence of knowing that You have not abandoned them. You are faithful to finish what You have started. Give them the strength, I pray; to dig deep, uprooting every tie and every bondage that has held them back. We take authority over fear and shame, and we place them under the blood of Jesus Christ. Let healing flow, now. In Jesus' name. Amen.

CHAPTER 9

Covenants, Vows, Allegiances & Alliances

God is a legal and just God. Throughout time, He has worked through established covenants in the earth, and history teaches us that He is always faithful to honor even those covenants we make with others. When we willfully enter into covenants, vows, allegiances, and alliances, we become bound by them and tied to those relationships or even entities. Even though God is supreme and sovereign, He will never violate the free will and power of choice which He gave Man; therefore, when we enter into covenants, vows, allegiances, and alliances—whether for our good or our bad— God will always honor them.

When we invite God into the arena of our lives to do something on our behalf, He is looking to see what contracts or agreements are in place, because these will determine the extent to which He can involve Himself in our affairs. Covenants, vows, allegiances, and alliances constitute legal agreements between two or more parties. These kinds of agreements establish many factors and boundaries against which God cannot and will not assert His will, until such time as we decide to renounce them and terminate the agreement. God is a legal God! And He is limited in His ability to move in our lives based on agreements we have made.

POWER OF AGREEMENT & ALIGNMENT

In this section, I want to deal with four very powerful words, all of which affect our ability to walk out our destiny. They are:

♦ Allegiance

♦ Alliance

♦ Agreement

♦ Alignment

"Again I say to you, that if two of you agree on earth about anything that they may ask, it shall be done for them by My Father who is in heaven."

Matthew 18:19

The underlying principle of the power of agreement is when two people agree on anything in the earthly realm, God is bound to honor it. This principle can also be applied to ungodly or unhealthy soul ties. If two people are walking in agreement outside of the bounds of the perfect will of God, it is still agreement and it is still a binding contract.

"Now I exhort you, brethren, by the name of our Lord Jesus Christ, that you all agree and that there be no divisions among you, but that you be made complete in the same mind and in the same judgment."

1 Corinthians 1:10

When two parties enter into a binding agreement, there is a unification that is constituted, causing those parties, according to this scripture, to become completely *one*, having the same *mind* and *judgment*. In other words, their thoughts, their discernment (or lack thereof), their sense of judgment, their ability to process ideas and problems and their decision-making abilities; they all become as one. Therefore, while I am trying to function with wisdom and understanding relating to the various aspects of my life, my business, my ministry, I find myself being limited to the mindset, thoughts, and judgments of the parties with which I have entered into an agreement. In principle then, when we align ourselves with the wrong people, the wrong group, the wrong businesses, or wrong institutions, we become unduly influenced by the deci-

> I am only able to succeed to the degree that the entity or person I am in agreement with succeeds. Their limitations become my limitations.

sions and beliefs of those parties. In other words, when we walk in agreement with someone, our thinking and how we process things in our own world is being affected by, if not controlled by, a spiritual force working in and through someone or something outside of ourselves.

An example of this that is very common in our world today is the gang culture. Young men and women, who for various reasons struggle with their own identity and self-worth, are many times drawn into this "community" called a gang. One of the steps involved in becoming a part of a gang family is the process of pledging one's allegiance to the gang and its objectives and mission. It is required that the prospective gang member in essence, pledge or sell their soul—that is, their independent intellect, thoughts, beliefs, values, culture, will, and emotions—into subservience to the thoughts, beliefs, values, and culture of the gang.

> Be careful who and what you align yourself with. It shapes and affects every area of your life.

This kind of agreement constitutes a legitimate soul tie. Many times these children come from middle to upper class families, being afforded all the advantages and opportunities for a normal and successful life. But over time, their own individual identity is absorbed or assimilated into the context and identity of the group with which the soul tie exists, producing a false sense of loyalty and security. Their life begins to mirror the chaos, confusion, anger, and destructive patterns that the corporate entity thrives on.

The same holds true of any allegiance, alliance, or vow we make in our lives. Be it personal, business, church, or any other arena, once we have joined ourselves to the arrangement by way of a contract or covenant, we begin to feel and experience the effects of that relationship on an altogether different level. It is critically important then to know and fully understand the environment and characteristics of anything or anyone with which we are considering entering into a covenant, vow, allegiance, or alliance. Be careful who and what you align yourself with. It shapes and affects every area of your life.

By definition, an "alliance" is a *treaty or covenant formed between individuals, groups, nations, or a businesses, which is designed to be mutually beneficial to all parties involved.* In Biblical times, a covenant or alliance was sealed by the blood of a sacrificial victim. The animal being sacrificed was cut into two pieces, causing the blood to be spilled out onto the ground between the pieces. Then, in a powerful and holy ceremony, the persons contracting the alliance or covenant would walk between the pieces, symbolizing the two becoming one (Genesis 15:10).

In some instances, there were alliances formed called "covenants of salt" (Numbers 18:19; 2 Chronicles 13:5); salt being the symbol of perpetuity. Throughout their entire history, the Jewish people attached great importance to fidelity to these covenants, and held them to be of tremendous importance and significance to their lives and futures. Let's continue now by looking at another aspect of the power of agreement.

Ox or Ass?

"Thou shalt not plow with an ox and an ass together."

Deuteronomy 22:10 (KJV)

This is a very powerful principle. It is apparent that God is showing us something here that has to do with an incompatible (or unholy) alignment. We know that when determining who you can walk with, the Bible instructs us to not be unequally yoked together. You cannot yoke up with someone who will ultimately work against you.

An ox is a serving animal with a sacrificial nature: it is willing to work, to be teachable, to submit to authority and counsel. An ass, on the other hand, has a rebellious, stubborn, and contrary nature. It is constantly fighting, rebelling, pulling against, disagreeing, and wearing you out. So many times in our lives, we enter into agreements or contracts with people whose nature is contrary to ours, and even to God's plans and purposes. They are obdurate and stubborn, refusing to work with God or work with you.

When we as Believers are living as sons of God and working to have our lives align with God's plans and purposes for our lives, we cannot afford to be aligned with, or walking in covenant with, someone with an ass spirit. We cannot afford to be in constant turmoil and struggle, fighting against something that is unwilling to move in the direction God desires to lead us. In business, we cannot afford to partner with or work with people whose values and morals are contrary to our

140

own. We cannot allow ourselves to be enticed into yoking up with people who are bitter, angry, dishonest, and cruel. This is a hopeless scenario! The ox and the ass cannot work together. It is counterproductive. It is a dangerous arrangement; one in which someone will always be hurt in the end. When we align ourselves with someone or something that is not walking the same direction as we are, we create the very mechanism that will impede us from ever reaching where it is we are trying to go.

Vows

Vows—like covenants, allegiances, and alliances—are binding agreements. They're binding in the spirit as well as in the natural. Vows can be made concerning people, entities, organizations, institutions, or things. You can even make a vow to yourself. Inner vows can be just as powerful in your life as vows made concerning others. They cause you to have a resolve either in a positive way or in a negative way.

Relationships: Growing up you may have had troubles, hurts, and pains that you experienced as a child or a teenager and have said to yourself, "I will never be like that again!" or "I will never let myself to be hurt like that again!" Maybe you said, "I will never let anybody get close to me, ever again!" You made an inner vow that created a soul tie to a spiritual dimension that is causing you all kinds of grief right now, today. You wonder why you have such difficulty receiving love; establishing or maintaining friendships or relationships. In the soulish realm, you have blocked off that part of you in order to defend your emotions. You have created a soul tie to a thought that, again, has you locked into a particular level of success.

141

Church experiences: If you have ever been wounded by religion or religious people, you may have made a vow that you will never, ever give your heart and soul to another church again. "I will never trust another pastor again!" Maybe you vowed never to be involved in ministry again because of the hurt you experienced. The consequences of that vow will continue producing detrimental and destructive fruit in your life, and because of this you can never fully engage in what God has for you. Regardless of the anointing and integrity on a man of God's life under whose ministry you may be sitting today, that vow you made will keep you from receiving the message of life he brings.

What if you were diagnosed with a life-threatening disease or sickness? The first thing we know to do, especially as Believers, is to call for the pastor or the elders of the church to pray and believe with us. If ever you needed to trust the man of God to believe God with you, now would be the time. They can pray, but that vow you made, if not dealt with and broken, will still be operating in your life and will keep you from receiving the complete and total healing and wholeness Jesus already paid the price for.

Marriage: Marriage vows are declarations of commitment and dedication between a man and a woman. God established the institution of marriage and He is a God of covenant. If you are married, you need to understand that you have made a covenantal vow before God and before man. That vow of marriage makes you one with your spouse. Concerning divorce, God takes it very seriously because it involves breaking a vow and a covenant. Even though you were divorced before you got saved or went through a divorce after being saved, you must deal with the soul ties resulting from those covenantal vows made with your previous spouse.

It is, then, imperative that you identify:

◆ With what or with who am I aligned?

◆ Have I yoked myself by agreement to a person or entity that is not traveling in the same direction as my destiny?

◆ What covenants, vows, allegiances, alliances, agree‑ ments, or alignments have I made, possibly years ago, that are still pulling on me?

◆ Have I made any inner vows that I need to repent of?

THE POWER OF A VOICE

In Genesis Chapter 1, God showed us the creative power in words when He *said*, ***"Let there be light,"*** and light *was* (Gen‑ esis 1:3). Scripture is jam-packed with examples of the creative power of words. Not only are words creative, but they also are life-giving. Words created the first life in the first of God's creatures, and also spoke new life into things that were dead.

Consider this:

"So they removed the stone. Then Jesus raised His eyes, and said, 'Father, I thank You that You have heard Me. {42} I knew that You always hear Me; but

because of the people standing around I said it, so that they may believe that You sent Me.' {43} When He had said these things, He cried out with a loud voice, 'Lazarus, come forth.' {44} The man who had died came forth, bound hand and foot with wrappings, and his face was wrapped around with a cloth. Jesus said to them, 'Unbind him, and let him go.'"

John 11:41-44

In this passage, Jesus, standing at the opening of the tomb of His close friend, called for Lazarus to come forth—and out came Lazarus, walking, still bound in grave clothes. By the power of His spoken words, Jesus broke the bond of death that was keeping Lazarus in the tomb.

But just as Jesus used his voice to speak life, He also used it to curse and to speak death.

"Now in the morning, when He was returning to the city, He became hungry. {19} Seeing a lone fig tree by the road, He came to it and found nothing on it except leaves only; and He said to it, 'No longer shall there ever be any fruit from you.' And at once the fig tree withered. {20} Seeing this, the disciples were amazed and asked, 'How did the fig tree wither all at once?'"

Matthew 21:18-20

Just as Lazarus' body responded to the life-giving power of Jesus' words, the fig tree responded to their negative, life-zapping power. Covenants, vows, allegiances, alliances, agree-

144

ments, and alignments constitute powerful and influential soul ties that are formed through **words**. Spoken words of agreement, allegiance, or alliance have all the validity and strength as do written contracts. Do not be lax in this area. It is too vital for your continued healing and restoration to be taken lightly.

WHO ARE YOU LISTENING TO?

"There are, it may be, so many kinds of voices in the world, and no kind is without signification."

1 Corinthians 14:10 (ASV)

Throughout the course of your life, there are constantly going to be voices speaking to you, vying for your attention, and drawing on you for a response. There will be those who always feel the need to add their "two cents worth" to your life. People are always going to be asking you to, "Come over here," "Do this with me," "Hook up with me," "Partner with me," or "Hang out with me." Although all voices have significance, not all of them are ones you should connect with.

If you are a business person, called by God to build and to prosper, you will always have opportunities (voices) presenting themselves to you. It is so important to distinguish between these voices. While every voice has significance, not every voice is the voice of God leading you to embrace an opportunity. Consider this scripture:

"But he who enters by the door is a shepherd of the sheep. {3} To him the doorkeeper opens, and the sheep hear his voice, and he calls his own sheep by name and

145

leads them out. {4} When he puts forth all his own, he goes ahead of them, and the sheep follow him because they know his voice. {5} A stranger they simply will not follow, but will flee from him, because they do not know the voice of strangers."

John 10:2-5

There are some voices that will lead you astray. There are forces at work in this world that desire to move you far away from the path God has called you to walk. These voices work with intent and diligence to distract and to discourage you. You must learn to discern the difference between those voices that will hinder you and those voices that will help you as you aspire to move into the destiny God has determined for you. The Bible says, *"My sheep hear My voice, and I know them, and they follow Me,"* (John 10:27).

Today are you following God's voice in your life, or are you still following after an old voice?

THE BINDING POWER OF YOUR VOICE

Your voice is as powerful as any voice in the earth. When you begin to hear what God has said about you, and you begin to say what He is saying, you enter into **agreement** with Him. When you and God agree, everything is possible.

"With the fruit of a man's mouth his stomach will be satisfied; He will be satisfied with the product of his lips."

Proverbs 18:20

What you say determines the fruit that is produced. When you join in agreement or make a covenant with someone or something or make a vow about yourself, someone else or something, you are going to produce fruit according to those words. If you don't like the fruit you see in your life, don't complain about it. Go back and analyze what has been coming out of your mouth. Your voice is powerful and your words are binding.

Many times Believers start fussing at God because things aren't turning out the way we think they should. We need to realize that somewhere along the way we may have vocally come into agreement with the wrong **voice** or said something that has put some things in motion in our life that are producing negative fruit. Remember, the fruit produced in your life is a direct result of what proceeds from your mouth.

Take heed from Scripture and do not make the mistake of underestimating the power of your words.

"Death and life are in the power of the tongue, and those who love it will eat its fruit."

Proverbs 18:21

This scripture could not be any more straight-forward. Your voice is a powerful and creative force in your life and in the lives of those around you. Covenants, vows, allegiances, and alliances are formulated and ratified by the things we speak. In fact, some covenants and vows can be formed even without you realizing it. Think before you speak!

THE CONSEQUENCES OF VIOLATING COVENANTS

The Bible tells us that when we have made covenants, vows, allegiances, and alliances, and we try to move in a direction that is contrary to those, there is a heavy price to pay.

> *"The sons of Israel did not strike them because the leaders of the congregation had sworn to them by the LORD the God of Israel. And the whole congregation grumbled against the leaders."*

> **Joshua 9:18**

> *"Now there was a famine in the days of David for three years, year after year; and David sought the presence of the LORD. And the LORD said, 'It is for Saul and his bloody house, because he put the Gibeonites to death.' {2} So the king called the Gibeonites and spoke to them (now the Gibeonites were not of the sons of Israel but of the remnant of the Amorites, and the sons of Israel made a covenant with them, but Saul had sought to kill them in his zeal for the sons of Israel and Judah)."*

> **2 Samuel 21:1-2**

> *"'As I live,' declares the Lord GOD, 'Surely in the country of the king who put him on the throne, whose oath he despised and whose covenant he broke, in Babylon he shall die.'"*

> **Ezekiel 17:16**

It is apparent throughout Scripture that God takes oaths and allegiances very seriously. Not only is this a warning, but it is also a comfort. Will He not take just as seriously His covenant with you and I established by the blood of Christ? God cannot violate a covenant He has made with Mankind. This is good news for Believers who have trusted in the redemptive act of Christ!

CLOSING THOUGHTS

So, you see, the ties that we form through covenants and alliances, vows and agreements, either written, spoken—even the inner vow that was spoken by you to yourself—bind us to the limited and unfruitful functionality of the past and of those people or entities we are tied to. In the case of the inner vow, you may have bound yourself emotionally to circumstances that should be ancient history; circumstances that you cannot allow to impose upon your present and your future.

Are you willing to allow an old covenant or alliance keep you stuck in your current state of success? Are you willing to continue to subject yourself to the terms and conditions of a contract that was ungodly and unhealthy to begin with? **Your answer must be a resounding "No!"** You must be free of these ties, so that you may begin to experience the fullness and scope of what God wants to release in your life.

No doubt you are beginning to recognize areas in which these types of ties are affecting your life. I am quite confident that God is speaking to you and revealing things even now. Take the time right now to journal some of what you are becoming aware of. Use the ideas below as a guide:

♦ *What relationships am I aware of that I presently am engaged with that would be "unequal" or "destructive" in nature?*

♦ *What covenants, vows, allegiances, and alliances have I made that are keeping me from realizing my destiny and my purpose being fulfilled?*

♦ *Am I still yoked with past business arrangements, a church, a friend that is limiting my forward progress?*

♦ *Be specific, be clear, and be honest as God is leading you through this process.*

You are doing great. You may feel a little pressure, a little resistance, but don't give up. God is with you. He is helping you. This knowledge is empowering you to be free. Let's keep working together!

Father, thank You for understanding. We know that You are bringing light to so many areas in our lives, and we welcome this challenge. We want to be free, and we want to know what it feels like to walk without limitations. Continue now, Lord, to give us the grace to be honest, and the courage to address these areas. We ask this in Your name. Amen.

Section III

The
Process

CHAPTER 10

Understanding the Process

At this point in the journey, I feel it is important to help you understand how this process is likely unfolding. By now, no doubt, you are experiencing a number of emotions, feelings, and possibly a measure of pain relating to some of the things you are identifying as soul ties in your life. You see, soul ties will keep us doing the same things while somehow, we assume that things are going to get better and our situations will change and turn around. Someone once said that insanity is "doing the same thing over and over expecting different results." In many ways, this is true. So many times we bury these things, or simply ignore them, hoping that they will simply "go away" or that time will somehow change things.

I have some bad news for you: soul ties don't just go away. They don't go away with time or distance. The saying, "Time heals all wounds," couldn't be farther from the truth. The real truth of the matter is a wound not tended to and left to itself can become septic and cause a serious infection, which ultimately affects the entire body. The effects of wounds and ungodly soul ties don't lessen if you merely ignore them. You can't wish them away or expect them to fix themselves. They don't go away with age or maturity. Not even disassociating yourself with people or things will automatically rid you of a soul tie.

Only by identifying unhealthy and ungodly soul ties operating in your life, acknowledging them, and willfully breaking them will you be free and allowed to move forward in power and strength; unrestricted by anything from your past. If you choose to do nothing, they will continue to draw on your life and cause you pain and sorrow.

A Preview of Things to Come – What to Expect

In reading through the previous pages, you may already have begun to recognize the "symptoms" of soul ties—maybe even in your own life. If for some reason you haven't yet, just buckle your seat belt. If you are willing to do what it takes to break the soul ties off of your life and allow God to reveal the symptoms and their sources, you can be assured that He will help you do that.

Understanding the process—and it is a process—is extremely important when dealing with soul ties. Below, I have listed several internal and external characteristics and feelings you may begin to experience while dealing with the severing of ungodly soul ties. You may already be experiencing some of them. If so, you may sense them becoming more intense as you move further into the materials in this book. You may experience various emotions or feelings, such as crying, anger, or feeling torn. In any event, just know this: as you begin to pursue your personal freedom, Satan desires to make it difficult for you.

Let me now share with you a few things you can likely expect when going through the process of breaking soul ties.

1. **Resistance.** This resistance is not only resistance from people. It can be resistance from spirits that are fighting to keep you down. It is resistance from those shackles, yokes, bondages, and chains—those soul ties. Satan knows that as long as we are held captive by the ties that bind us, we are vulnerable and make for an easy target.

2. **Sorrow or grief.** You may experience increased sorrow or grief. The feelings may be as subtle as being sad; having lost your joy, your song, or your smile, but not knowing why. It may feel like you have just lost a good friend, or you could have more intense feelings of grief and loss, like the loss of a loved one, or as though you have experienced a death in your life. Remember, in breaking and cutting off ungodly soul ties, there is a cutting away from your life. The loss may actually be the intentional severing of a friendship, relationship, or a bad habit. Either way, the removal and extraction

of things in your life that have caused the soul ties can sometimes be hard to bear.

3. **Anger.** Anger is an emotion that oftentimes manifests out of conflict and pain. When individuals have been abused or hurt in life and those situations go unaddressed and unresolved, those feelings lie dormant; festering and becoming toxic. When we begin to stir things up and uncover things, many times our emotions are expressed through anger. We become irritable, quick-tempered, and some people even become aggressive. We must pray that God will help us to curb these emotions as we progress toward our freedom.

4. **Above-average frustration.** We feel as if nothing is going right. Sometimes we can even feel hopeless, as if we can never be free. Several times in my own journey, I felt as if I could never be free; never be whole; never be able to BE the man God called me to be. I found that I had to focus on the outcome I **knew** God had for me, and not allow Satan to talk me out of it. Frustration can be a good thing if channeled properly. It provides motivation to keep going!

5. **Fear.** The Bible says that God has not given us a spirit of fear, but rather, He has given us the spirit of POWER, LOVE, and a SOUND MIND. Fear paralyzes us. It causes us to lose sight of who we are and where we are going. Fear keeps us in a defensive posture, while God calls us on the offensive. The

Bible teaches us that we are to "take things by force," (Matthew 11:12). If you are dealing with fear, then you must know that Satan is working to keep you where you are. You have the power of God working for you; you have the love of God being graced upon you; you have access to the very mind of Christ.

6. **Anxiety – and above-average anxiety.** The Bible says in Philippians 4:6 to **"Be anxious for nothing."** When anxiety exists, you can rest assured that it is not coming from God. We feel anxious, many times, because we are in unfamiliar territory. When you have become used to a certain way of existing, as you challenge that your heart and mind are thrown out of order. This causes anxiety.

7. **Depression.** I have observed individuals who are walking out the process of dealing with these matters, and noticed that some tend to go into a depressive state. This is because our creative subconscious is always working to regulate what we **believe** to be true, with what we are seeing and moving toward. In other words, if we are pursuing freedom from a past relationship, vow, or soul tie, but on the inside we strongly believe that we should **not** break that connection, our mind and body will react, causing the symptoms of depression.

8. **Loss of motivation.** Loss of motivation comes in many different forms. You may feel as if your energy is drained or you're just "spent." You can't find or

capture passion for anything. You feel like you're just existing and in a spiritual and/or emotional coma. All you want to do is sleep, which is a classic symptom of depression, as well.

9. **Find it hard to pray.** Praying becomes a chore and you might not even *want* to pray. When you do—if you do—it seems useless and a waste because you feel nothing and are incapable of expecting anything; your prayers **feel** lifeless and faithless. Remember, God hears you. You may not feel as if you are getting through, but God is working.

10. **Deliverance issues.** This one always has the potential to make someone uncomfortable, but nonetheless, it is very real. When you're going through the process of breaking soul ties in your life, you may notice a deeper spiritual dilemma begin to manifest. When a person begins to yield their soul to the Word of God and begins to break away from long-standing bondages, the soul can feel as though it is in shock, and you know no other way to handle it than to cry out. Isaiah 58:1 tells us to "cry aloud." Sometimes if the **soulish** matter is deep-rooted enough, you may begin to deal with demonic spirits and curses that are embedded in your life as well. Remember, we are spirit, soul, and body. It is often the case that soul and spirit issues go hand in hand. Do not allow fear to keep you from going after total healing. It is God's desire for you to

be complete: body, soul, and spirit. Just allow God to do what He wants to in order to set you free!

THE POWER IN SOUL TIES

There are some soul ties that are so deeply rooted in the soul that they are woven literally into the very fabric of your spirit. That's why you feel what you feel. You have to understand that the emotions we feel originate from the region of our soul. That's why we feel depressed. That's why we feel sorrow. That's why we feel anger, frustration, and anxiety. All of those things are "soulish" things.

POWER SHORTAGE

When I was teaching on soul ties at our church in Dallas, a man came up to me after a service and shared something that happened to him during the altar call when we were actually going through dealing with the soul ties. I thought it was a great visual example of the effects of soul ties operating in our lives and had him share it with the congregation. I think it's important enough to share it with you as well. "John," who is not the type of individual to normally have visions or experiences of this type, shared how he had spent several years in prison. Because of his time in jail, any and all relationships with women, ex-wives and such, were broken off. When we dealt with relational soul ties in our service, he initially felt that there were no issues in his life that needed to be addressed. As I asked everyone in the congregation to stand—even before the altar call—God gave him a very powerful vision, one that would forever change his life.

159

John saw a vision where he was a power source, and there were many electrical plugs that were plugged into him, drawing on him. They weren't the small 110-voltage plugs. Instead, they were the big, round, 220-volt plugs. He said, "I watched as these huge plugs were draining me of all my energy; and I was not even aware! I was blind to the fact that there were things pulling on me and taking from me. I couldn't see them. I didn't understand it." He shared with me that he watched as the other areas of his life 'dimmed' as these unwanted items were pulling on his energy.

Today, John is happily married and serving God. He said God began to show him how there were times in his marriage when the lights were dimming. He told our people how much he loved his wife and wanted to have a great marriage, yet he could see these other things pulling from him. What a great visual of the powerful effects of soul ties on our lives. Although a soul tie may just be in one area—or with one person, thing or situation—when it pulls on us, it affects every area of our life—not just that one area where the soul tie resides. Soul ties literally drain us of energy, power, strength, vision, faith, hope—you name it. They are enemies of our soul and can cause not only a power shortage, but in severe cases, complete power outages.

Paul tells us exactly what God desires for our life here:

"Now to Him who is able to do far more abundantly beyond all that we ask or think, according to the power that works within us."

Ephesians 3:20

160

Unfortunately, when most people quote this scripture, they leave off the most important part—the "according to the power that works within us." If we have unhealthy and ungodly soul ties drawing from us against our will, we have to ask ourselves, "How much power do I *really* have operating in me?" As Believers, we get our "power" from the Holy Spirit operating in us through our spirit man. But remember, when soul ties are working in our life, our spirit man takes a back seat to our soul, and our soul becomes the dominating force or power working in us.

ARE WE REALLY GOING TO THE NEXT LEVEL?

It's important to mention that soul ties may not affect us all the time. They may only affect us during certain seasons of our life. During seasons in our life when God is trying to get us to that next level, these soul ties begin to pull on us. Like that bungee cord, they hold us back from reaching our destiny and our purpose. They keep us down and stop us from going higher.

ALL IS NOT LOST

As you go through the process of breaking soul ties, it is very possible to feel like you are losing something. Some soul ties have been there for so long, unnoticed and not dealt with, that we have learned to live with them. We have adjusted our lives to their presence and have acclimated ourselves to them. We have become comfortable with them. We've even built a special room in our house just for them.

We are creatures of habit, and on the whole, we hate change. In order to avoid change, we have become accustomed to living with the abnormal. The thought of change or removing the soul ties leaves us with the misconception that there is going to be a void in us. Oddly enough, subconsciously, we process them this way.

In all actuality, God is really trying to remove something that is detrimental to our well-being. When God supernaturally removes something from our life, He always replaces it with something that is so much better. It may not feel like it at first, but in the end, it's always better! God is the giver of all good things. He wants the very best for His children.

Now, the Good News . . .

I personally understand how you are feeling right about now having read this far. I have been there. When God began to teach me about soul ties, and as I began to deal with my own—ones that, for years, I had no idea even existed—it was a gut-wrenching, difficult time in my life. Like all of us, I had a choice to make. I could have chosen to ignore them, but the next year, I would have found myself in the same exact place, still struggling and fighting. You are in that place right now. Realize that you are the author of your own destiny. Regardless of who we are or where we come from, we are never above the place where soul ties can latch on to us and affect our lives. But this is not the end of the story ... there's good news!

"For I am confident of this very thing, that He who began a good work in you will perfect it until the day of Christ Jesus."

Philippians 1:6

When God directs us to move into a season of dealing with soul ties, He doesn't promise that it is going to be easy. In fact, just the opposite is true. It is work, no doubt. We have to know that above all, God is completely committed to seeing it all the way through to the end. Whatever feelings you are experiencing now—and we mentioned them earlier: resistance, sorrow, anger, frustration, fear, anxiety, depression, loss of motivation, finding it hard to pray—and probably a million other verbs and adjectives, or a host of negative emotions you can name—God will see you to the end.

What is happening is that you are having a chiropractic adjustment of the God-kind! You are getting your spirit, soul, and body in alignment with the Word of God. In the end, it's all good! I'm telling you right now, from experience—and if you've ever visited a chiropractor, you know what I'm talking about. You can have one leg longer than the other. Is your leg really longer than the other one? No, of course it's not. It may look like it, but in actuality, it is that your spine is not aligned correctly, so it gives the appearance of your leg being a different length. The chiropractor doesn't work on making your leg longer. Instead, he works on your spine, which brings your entire body into proper function.

Now, here's the deal: If our soul has worked its way up to the head, then it's going to take a lot more than just a chiropractic adjustment to get it back where it's supposed to be. We have to get our spirit man back in the position to rule as headship over our life, as opposed to our soul driving us through life and keeping us in bondage to all these various emotions, problems, and issues.

Please, please, please understand what I am about to say to you right now. It is critical that you understand this. If God is committed to finishing this thing in us—and He is—we also have to be committed to finishing it with Him.

CHAPTER 11

Breaking the Ties that Bind

We have now come to a wonderful, yet critical cross-roads in our journey. For many people, the process of understanding the concept of soul ties and becoming aware of those ties in their own lives can prove to be difficult, if not downright painful. Recognizing and acknowledging the person, thing or event in your life that originally caused the formation of a soul tie in you has, no doubt, brought up memories, some of which you would rather not have to address. Issues that you thought were dead and buried have proven to be very much alive, and are affecting you in a detrimental way. As these matters surface, you may be finding that these holds on you are not easily broken, and some are determined to not go away without a fight.

For some of you, this may have brought up memories or feelings that have been hidden away in the dark crevices of our soul for many years. As hurtful as these memories are now, please believe me, this is not a bad thing. We have to allow those things to come to the surface so that we can deal with them and allow God to remove them. Remember this principle: Satan is the ruler of the darkness. What we place there willfully, he has the power and authority to rule in us. As the Holy Spirit brings these things to our awareness, we must willingly bring them into the light; it is **there** that God can and will deal with them once and for all.

> *"Confess your faults one to another, and pray one for another, that ye may be healed. The effectual fervent prayer of a righteous man availeth much."*

> **James 5:16 (KJV)**

A fault is a crack in the foundation. It is below the surface and is not seen by the natural eye. Consider how an earthquake is initiated. It begins due to a fault line running beneath the visible surface of the earth. Some event takes place, and there is a shifting of balance and the fault gives way to a quake, and many times, destruction follows.

This is the time to get real. It's time to be completely and totally honest with God and with yourself. You are the only one who can decide whether you will continue to live the way you have been—same result, same limitations, same problems, same challenges—or choose to address and break the power of the soul ties which hold you back, so that you may experience freedom you never knew was possible. It is a matter of your free will. Remember, God will not violate your will. However, if you choose to engage with what God is trying to do in you, I can promise and assure you, that He will complete the work He has begun, and it will be a perfect work!

"For I am confident of this very thing, that He who began a good work in you will perfect it until the day of Christ Jesus."

Philippians 1:6

"The Lord will accomplish what concerns me; Your lovingkindness, O Lord is everlasting; do not forsake the works of Your hands."

Psalm 138:8

Let me offer some very relevant insight at this point. Satan does not like the fact that he has been exposed. If you haven't already done so, I would suggest that you anoint and pray over your home; pray over your family; and cover things and people in your life by the blood of Jesus. You are now on the offensive, and you are literally taking back territory that belongs to you. Satan will try his best to fight you because of what you are doing. Just remember, "Greater is He that is in you, than he that is in the world!" (1 John 4:4, paraphrased). The Greater One lives inside you! Watch this!

"What then shall we say to these things? If God is for us, who is against us?"

Romans 8:31

Four Steps to Breaking Free

1. **You must want to be free.** It is not sufficient for someone to desire it for you. In the same respect, neither can you want someone else to be free more than they want it for themselves. I believe you have to come to the point where you desperately desire to be free. A powerful part of your soul is your will—something God will never violate. We must yield our will to God in order for us to receive what we want from Him.

2. **You must be willing to let go.** Many times we desire one thing, but are unwilling to let go of the old thing. Paul said, "Forgetting (releasing) what lies behind, and pressing for what is ahead," (Philippians 3:13, paraphrased). The Bible also teaches us that a double-minded man is unstable in all his ways (James 1:8). You must come to a point where you are willing to let go of those relationships, associations, covenants, emotions—all those things that you know are unhealthy or ungodly that have you bound.

   I remember a story I heard once about a group of hunters that were trying to capture a very elusive species of monkey. The hunters would devise and build traps and set them out in hope of capturing their prey. They would put fruit inside the trap, hoping that when the monkeys saw the fruit, they would go in to grab it and, "Voila!" it would be caught! Unfortunately for the hunters, the monkeys didn't fall for that. The monkeys were clever and would study the trap carefully. Finally, the little guys realized they could reach in and grab the fruit before the trap door even closed shut.

One day, one of the hunters had an idea that he thought could work to trap the monkeys. He built a box inside the trap, and he put the fruit inside the box. The front of the box had a small hole in it, just large enough for the monkey's hand to fit into. He set the trap with the box inside it out that night to see what would happen. The next morning, they came out to find the monkey stuck in the trap with his hand still inside the hole in the box.

You see, the monkey had reached in to grab the fruit, but when he clutched his fist around the fruit, his hand was now too big to take out of the hole in the box. All the monkey had to do was to let go of the fruit and he could have freed himself, but instead he was **holding on**. The monkey wanted that fruit badly! No doubt, the monkey, since he had avoided capture up to this point, did not want to be trapped. But it was his **"not letting go"**—his persistence in clutching the fruit—that, to him, seemed something worth hanging on to. This is what got him caught and proved to be the loss of, at the very least, his freedom, and quite possibly, his life.

God will always provide a way out of your situation, but you cannot escape without first letting go! We can't ask God to break the soul tie off of our life if **we** aren't willing to let go of it. Many times we pray, "God free me," when God is saying, "Free yourself."

One example of this "hanging on" is found in the possessions of sentimental items. I have learned through counseling people through the process of breaking soul ties that gifts we have received, items we shared with someone in days gone by, and other possessions can tie us to the past as well. We have to be careful that things such as gifts, trinkets, letters, songs, pictures don't prohibit us from being able to break free of soul ties.

I know a young woman who saved everything she was ever given from her high school sweetheart. The two had planned on getting married after their high school graduation, so she collected these sentimental things with the idea that one day they could be put in their scrapbooks so they could share the memories with their children and grandchildren. She had a virtual treasure trove of pictures, jewelry, clothing items, recordings of their favorite songs, love letters, cards, notes, years and years of journals, stuffed animals, and papers with the names of their future children written on them—you name it, she had it! Well, you know where I am going with this. Their relationship came to an end, but she decided she would hold onto those sentimental things; keeping them in boxes and bags.

Years later this young lady married another man, and their first two years of marriage were very tumultuous. Everything she had ever dreamed about marriage could not have been farther from her reality. When she and her husband would have bad arguments and fights, the husband would leave the house in a rage, and she would find herself dragging out her boxes of sentimental items from the previous relationship -- looking through the pictures and letters, listening to the music, wishing for a way out of her marriage. In these moments, she could feel the pull of that old world, and she would cry her eyes out in desperation.

She loved her husband but looking at those sentimental things and listening to music they used to listen to together, took her back to that time and kept her emotionally and mentally tied to that old relationship in her life. She began to realize that every time she went back to her sentimental boxes, the love for her husband dwindled more and more. She realized her marriage didn't stand a chance at surviving if she could not let go of everything she had from her past relationship.

With much difficulty, she threw everything away. She burned all her journals, pictures, letters— everything! She said it was literally like tearing a piece of her heart and soul out, and it was one of the hardest things she ever had done in her lifetime.

This young woman's marriage wasn't instantly healed. In fact, it was a long, hard road before she even saw fruits from that "cutting off" point. But by letting go of her past, she was finally in a position to have a fresh start and give herself one hundred percent to her marriage. God blessed it and she has been totally free from that soul tie ever since.

We cannot afford to have sentimental things keeping us bound and enslaved to our past, including past relationships. Get rid of them and you will experience yet another level of freedom!

3. **You must repent.** If you have an ungodly soul tie, then you have been disconnected from God in those areas, and therefore, it is sin. We have to repent of those things and repent of allowing them to rule our thoughts, our heart, our emotions, and our flesh. Paul puts it another way:

> *"For the mind set on the flesh is death, but the mind set on the Spirit is life and peace."*

> **Romans 8:6**

In order for us to get what God really wants us to have, we must repent: turn away from it and go the opposite direction.

4. **You must renounce the soul ties.** You may have heard the word "renounce" as meaning *to not agree with*, or *not believe in*; however, the word has a much stronger meaning. The actual dictionary definition according to Merriam-Webster is: *(1.) To give up, refuse, or resign usually by formal declaration and (2.) To refuse to follow, obey, or recognize any further."* [14] A word that can be used in conjunction with "renounce" is "repudiate," which means *to make a renunciation*. It also means *to refuse to have anything to do with, to refuse to accept and to reject something as being unauthorized or as having no binding force, to refuse to acknowledge and to refuse to make a payment*.[15]

Another powerful synonym for "renounce" is "abdicate." Abdicate means *to cast off and to relinquish (as sovereign power) formally, and to renounce a throne, high office, dignity, or function.*[16] That is so powerful!

Merriam-Webster goes on to say that both words "renounce" and "abdicate" mean, *to give up a position with no possibility of resuming it*. Abdicate implies *a giving up of sovereign power*,[17] but the word *renounce may replace it [abdicate] or often implies additionally a sacrifice for a greater end.* [18]

It may feel like we are "giving up" something in the natural, but in all reality, we are breaking off and

---

[14] http://www.m-w.com/dictionary/renounce
[15] http://www.m-w.com/dictionary/repudiate
[16] http://www.m-w.com/dictionary/abdicate
[17] Ibid
[18] Ibid

renouncing those soul ties in exchange for God's perfect will and blessings to be manifested in our lives.

On the flip side of that, let me explain it to you from a different view. Merriam-Webster gives this as an example of the exact meaning of this word. Watch this!

[She] "renounced her inheritance by marrying a commoner."[19]

This is so powerful! We have to remember one thing: We are always speaking out against something—good or bad. If we speak out *for* marriage between one man and one woman, then we are speaking out *against* same-sex marriages. If we speak out *against* abortion, we are speaking *for* human life. Using Merriam-Webster's great example, the woman spoke out her vows declaring her love and life *for* a commoner—a term used in medieval times to describe a person who was not of noble birth. In doing so, she also spoke out *against* and "renounced" her inheritance.

As heirs to the King, being sons and daughters of God, we have a divine inheritance that grants us full access to the Kingdom—the wealth, the riches, the blessings, the health, the joy, the peace—and everything that comes with it. However, when we

---

[19] http://www.m-w.com/dictionary/renounce

refuse to renounce ungodly soul ties in our life, then we are renouncing our inheritance

We must declare in an audible statement that we renounce any and all ungodly soul ties and decree our freedom from all binding obligations to past agreements. **We have to <u>say</u> it!** It is a legal declaration in the spirit that seals the finality of a thing. Our mouth is the instrument that we are instructed by God to use to disconnect us, once and for all, from the ties that bind.

5. **We have to receive.** You ask, "What do we have to receive?" First of all, we have to receive the grace of God. Secondly, we have to receive His love and forgiveness. Thirdly, we receive restoration. When you break free from an ungodly soul tie, you now stand in alignment to receive restoration of everything that was lost as a result of that soul tie. This is retroactive and without limitation. Whatever that relational soul tie has stolen from you over the years, God says that He will restore all things back to you. We have to receive total and complete freedom in our life. By doing so, we receive the fullness of God's plan for our life.

> *"So rejoice, O sons of Zion, and be glad in the LORD your God; for He has given you the early rain for your vindication and He has poured down for you the rain, the early and latter rain as before. {24} The threshing floors will be full*

of grain, and the vats will overflow with the new wine and oil. {25} Then I will make up to you for the years that the swarming locust has eaten, the creeping locust, the stripping locust and the gnawing locust, My great army which I sent among you. {26} You will have plenty to eat and be satisfied and praise the name of the LORD your God, Who has dealt wondrously with you; then My people will never be put to shame. {27} Thus you will know that I am in the midst of Israel, and that I am the LORD your God, and there is no other; and My people will never be put to shame."

Joel 2:23-27

YOUR REVIEW

At this point in your process of releasing soul ties, I need you to get all of your thoughts and notes from previous chapters or journals that you may have written in as you were going through this book together. No doubt you have identified numerous ties that you believe God is going to free you from today. Take those now, and organize them into an easy to follow format allowing you to address them one by one as we go through the prayer process. Important elements to consider may be:

♦ Name of a person

♦ Words spoken or shared

- Covenants made

- Sexual or non-sexual in nature

- Churches, spiritual leaders

- Associations, business relationships

- Social or service club memberships

- Inner vows

THE PRAYER

You're almost there! Before you pray this prayer, I want to remind you that healing, restoration, and victory are in your very near future. God's love, grace, mercy, and power are available to you. It is His greatest desire that our soul prospers.

"Beloved, I pray that in all respects you may prosper and be in good health, just as your soul prospers."

3 John 2

The King James says, "I wish above all things."

Now, as you have written notes throughout reading this book—i.e. things, people, events, and situations—call them out individually in prayer when the time comes.

LET'S PRAY!

"Father, in the name of Jesus, I come to You with an open heart, a spirit that cries aloud to be free. I acknowledge that I need You, and that I have been

bound by soul ties that have been hurtful to my relationship with You and with others. In this very moment, more than anything, I desire to be free of EVERY tie that would hinder Your ability to release me into my full destiny. Lord, I am desperate. I cannot go another day in this condition.

Of my own will, I let go of my hold to every unhealthy relationship, allegiance, alliance, and tie that is affecting my life. I choose this day to release myself and others from any and all obligations or contracts made that involve my spirit, my soul, or my body."

Name Them . . .

I repent of every sin that I have committed that has caused me to be bound in my life. I repent of allowing my soul to rule my life instead of Your Spirit working in me. I repent of yielding my mind and my heart to relationships that are unhealthy. I repent of yoking myself together with people, places, and things that have created strain and frustration. This day, I choose to turn and walk away from every tie that has bound me in any area of my life.

Name Them . . .

I renounce every soul tie, every covenant, every agreement, every contract, and every yoke. By the authority of Jesus Christ, I cancel every debt, every obligation, and every ungodly connection that exists in my life. I cancel the effects of every threat, every lie, every deceit, and every curse that has been spoken to me, about me, or for me. From this day on, I will not receive the consequences of these ties, nor will I allow any of these relationships to collect from me. I apply the blood of Jesus to every aspect of my life and I declare with authority that Satan no longer has the right to affect my life.

Name Them

Now, Lord God, I receive the freedom that you have promised me in Your Word. I receive the grace, the love, the joy, and the peace that is mine by inheritance. Everything that I have lost and everything that has been stolen from me must now be returned to me with interest. I call on complete restoration and remediation. I am free! I am whole! I am restored! Most of all, my soul belongs to You! I am free!

Final Thoughts

What an incredible journey! You have no doubt discovered (and maybe uncovered) some very powerful things that have been holding you back. God has revealed to you many areas where you have been bound by ungodly and unhealthy soul ties. You have faced them head-on and now . . . FREEDOM! Freedom from bondage; freedom from unnecessary limitations; freedom from emotional and spiritual ties that have been keeping you stuck in a pattern of brokenness and recurring cycles. Today, those limitations no longer have claim to your soul. They no longer have the right or the power to collect from you or pull on you. What an exciting place to be!

WHERE DO YOU GO FROM HERE?

I know that by now you have experienced a true encounter with a loving God, so first, let me tell you that the freedom you are experiencing right now is yours for keeps. You have applied the principles and truths of God's Word, and His promise of freedom is yours. Satan may try to convince you that you are not free, but remember, the devil is a liar!

"So if the Son makes you free, you will be free indeed."

John 8:36

Toward the beginning of this teaching, I shared with you that healing is a process. While we celebrate the wonderful freedom that you are now experiencing, we must know that there will be other areas that God will systematically reveal, and provide you the opportunity to continue the healing journey. Someone once said that healing is like peeling the layers of an onion. In a particular season, God gives us the understanding and the grace to deal with a certain "layer," and with that grace, we find healing and freedom in *that* area. Maybe we go several years, enjoying our new-found freedom, only to find that God introduces us to more information or more revelation, and provides us with the opportunity to deal with yet another area altogether. So layer by layer, we go through life receiving the healing and restoration God so desires us to walk in. It truly is faith to faith, glory to glory.

In our world today, there are so many causative factors that bring a person into bondage: abandonment, abuse (sexual, emotional, spiritual), traumatic experiences, curses (generational, spoken, self-imposed)—and so many others. In this book, we have dealt primarily with *Soul Ties*. I have found that when you begin to undo long-standing or deep-rooted soul ties, many times you will uncover related issues in other areas.

Remember, our goal is to be whole: body, soul, and spirit. As we uproot things in the soul, spiritual and physical elements may be stirred up and exposed.

By no means am I trying to discourage you by bringing these to your attention. To the contrary, my desire is to encourage you. You have successfully navigated and processed one of the most important components of the healing process. Now, I want to encourage you to continue the journey. Allow God to lead you step by step.

Your life is scripted by God. He has a magnificent plan for you. You are fearfully and wonderfully made. It is so important that you put the past behind you and look forward. Begin to see clearly what lies ahead. Your future is set in God's heart. The Scripture says that God knows the plans He has for you: *"'For I know the plans that I have for you,' declares the LORD, 'plans for welfare and not for calamity to give you a future and a hope,'"* **(Jeremiah 29:11)**. The only limitations that will keep us from realizing that future are the ones we allow to hold us. Take this new-found freedom and go BE the man or woman God created you to be.

> *"'Before I formed you in the womb I knew you; before you were born I sanctified you; I ordained you a prophet to the nations.' {6} Then said I: 'Ah, Lord GOD! Behold, I cannot speak, for I am a youth.' {7} But the LORD said to me: 'Do not say, 'I am a youth,' For you shall go to all to whom I send you, And whatever I command you, you shall speak. {8} Do not be afraid of their faces, for I am with you to deliver*

you,' says the LORD. *{9} Then the* LORD *put forth His hand and touched my mouth, and the* LORD *said to me: 'Behold, I have put My words in your mouth.{10} See, I have this day set you over the nations and over the kingdoms, to root out and to pull down, to destroy and to throw down, to build and to plant.'"*

Jeremiah 1:5-10

About the Author

Brian Holmes lives in the Dallas/Ft. Worth area with his wife, Sabrina, and their two children, Christian and Abigail. Brian and Sabrina are the founders and overseers of Covenant International Worship Center, a dynamic growing ministry center in the Dallas/Ft. Worth area.

Brian is also the founder and president of Church Strategies International and is certified as a church analyst and consultant. His ministry is "apostolic in nature" with an emphasis on reforming and empowering the Church to walk in power and authority. His passion is to equip and empower pastors, leaders, and lay persons to be released into their complete purpose and destiny; thereby, establishing the Kingdom of God in the earth. Each year, Brian travels extensively speaking and ministering in churches, crusades, and leadership forums both in the United States and around the world.

Contact Information

For more information about Brian A. Holmes Ministries,
or to invite Brian Holmes to speak for your church, ministry,
or organization, you may contact our offices at the number
below, or simply write, fax, or e-mail a letter of invitation to
one of the following contacts provided below.

Brian Holmes Ministries
445 E. FM 1382, Suite 3-377
Cedar Hill, Texas 75104 USA
469.272.7300 phone
469.574.5040 fax

e-mail: info@baholmes.com
online: www.baholmes.com
www.ciwc.net

More Products Available From Brian Holmes

The Quest for Authentic Leadership
8 Audio CD Series

If ever we have needed a generation of authentic leaders, it is NOW. We have arrived in the 21st century only to realize that our world is lacking in the area of Godly and principle centered leadership. In our schools, our government, our churches, and even our homes, there is a void that must be filled.

In this series, Pastor Holmes addresses the idea that in order for us to realize the destiny in our own lives, and that of our respective nations, we must restore the principles of Biblical and Godly leadership. He addresses ideas such as: personal responsibility, ownership and accountability, governing values, personal discipline, honesty and integrity, time management, goals and dreams, and so much more,

This series will equip you to become the leader that God created you to be, and inspire you to elevate your commitment to personal development and growth. Titles include: An Introduction to Authentic Leadership; Character Qualifications of Authentic Leadership-Part One; Character Qualifications of Authentic Leadership-Part Two; The Process of Leadership Development; Discovering Your Personal Leadership Identity; Discovering Your Purpose; The Qualifications of Leadership; and Leadership Attitudes.

The Solomon Generation
5 Audio CD Series

King David is about to die, and there must be a legitimate successor for his throne. Adonijah bypasses the system, and sets himself up as king, even though he was not anointed and chosen. Before David dies, he sees to it that Solomon, his chosen one, is anointed and established as king.

This is the picture of what is happening in the earth even now. A generation is passing, and God is in need of a Solomon generation to rise up and be established in the earth to build Him a house. This generation is one with tremendous understanding and breadth of mind. It is a generation that has been chosen by our Father to represent Him as legitimate, anointed sons in the earth. God is raising such a generation!

In this 5 disc series, Pastor Brian Holmes delivers a message that will awaken the Solomon anointing in you. Message titles include: King for a Day; Anointed to be King; The House of Solomon; Solomon's Desire; and Solomon's Destiny Fulfilled. This series will cause you to reign as God's chosen in the earth.

The Ties That Bind
6 Audio CD Series

This powerful 6-CD audio series offers instruction concerning the consequences and detrimental effects of unhealthy and ungodly soul ties. Since we were created in the image of God, we are Body, Soul, and Spirit. It is the SOUL of an individual that often times finds itself in disarray, thus, never allowing that person to fully experience a satisfied and productive life. This series will change your life and set you free.

The Spirit of Excellence
6 Audio CD Series

Excellence is that quality that causes a person to rise above average and ordinary; to move beyond the limitations of a commonplace, status quo existence. Excellence is actually a spirit...an attitude. The difference between good and great is not something enormous and insurmountable...it is in the little things. God has designed you in His image, and in His likeness, and He is calling us to a lifestyle of EXCELLENCE. He is looking for sons to rise and represent His excellence and greatness in the earth.

A Message to the Church
8 Audio CD Series

In this series, Pastor Holmes give the listener a powerful viewpoint on God's messages to the seven churches in Revelation chapters 1-3. Revelation 1:6 says,"And He has made us to be a KINGDOM...". This is the purpose for which we were created. This is the sole objective of the church. As the series unfolds, we begin to see that the issues in the church today are addressed very clearly and succinctly in these writings to the seven churches. Some of these include; the loss first love; suffering and testing; false teachings; idolatry; immortality; the spirit of Jezebel; dead vision; keys of access and open doors; lukewarmness; and many more. God is calling His church to address these issues, overcome them, and be restored to our assigned place in the Kingdom. This series will challenge you to rise up, repent, overcome and take your place. It will empower you to BE the Kingdom.

Curses
8 Audio CD Series

"See, I am setting before you this day, a blessing and a curse..."

Deuteronomy 11:26

There are forces at work in our lives that can cause us to function at levels far beneath the plan and destiny that God has set for us, and many times we have no conscience knowledge of their origin or source. These forces and systems rob us of our ability to walk in health, freedom, victory, joy, and fullness. Many times, these issues are related to CURSES that have been passed down through generations, or brought on by our own sin and disobedience. The important thing to know is that God gave us a choice...blessing or curse.

In this series, Brian Holmes opens the Word of God in a systematic teaching on the subject of CURSES. Titles include: An Introduction to Curses; Generational/Bloodline Curses; Occult/Witchcraft Curses; Spoken Word/Self Imposed Curses; The Curse of the Bastard Spirit; and in the final session, Pastor Brian leads us step by step, prayer by prayer, and proclamation by proclamation through the process of Breaking Curses. The information contained in these teachings is both timely and profound, and will give you the knowledge, understanding, and tools to break free from the inhibiting forces in your life, once and for all!